# who put
# the con in
# consumer?

# who put the con in consumer?

## by david sanford

liveright · new york

1.987654321

International Standard Book Number: 0-87140-550-4 (cloth)
International Standard Book Number: 0-87140-075-8 (paper)
Library of Congress Catalog Card Number: 70-184100

Liveright Paperbound Edition 1972

Designed by Elliot Epstein
Manufactured in the United States of America

*For my grandparents*
*Fritz and Alice Peterson*

# contents

# introduction

Someone who read the galleys of *Who Put the Con in Consumer?* prior to publication told me he thought it was an "amusing, opinionated book." I don't know whether to take that as a compliment. "Amusing" may be a nice way of saying that my purpose in writing the book did not seem to be serious, or that it's not a serious book. "Opinionated" might suggest that my conclusions are not verifiably true. I leave such judgments to the reader. I do think however that there is something to be said for a treatment of consumer subjects which is not as angry as Ralph Nader nor as dogmatic or self-righteous in its suggestions for how to tackle consumer problems. And I think there is a place for inferences as well as scientific proofs. I admit to believing, for example, that most business conducted in this country is so oriented toward making the highest legal profit that there is very little interest left in quality. Go to Paris and see how interested a restaurateur can be in delivering value for the dollar spent. If the courses you order strike the waiter as dissonant, or the wine is wrong, he may wince and tell you that you can't do that with your money. One has the distinct feeling that the French (forgive the unverifiable generalization) still care about craft as well as profit. I doubt that International Telephone and Telegraph's Wonder Bread division does much business in Paris. In corporate America, however, any innovation that will decrease the cost to a manufacturer and thereby increase the profit margin is likely to be tried unless the FDA steps in and says it causes cancer. Businessmen are very quick to point out that they do market

1

research to ascertain what people want to buy and that convenience and cost are paramount considerations. If Wonder Bread costs less and tastes all right, people will buy it. A "good" cookie is one a child will eat, not necessarily one made with butter and eggs and other natural ingredients. It's difficult to argue esthetics, but it seems to me that the quality of the things we buy is getting worse and that, as a result, the money we are all so eager to earn buys only cheap junk. Of course the President of General Motors, with his six-figure salary, has more options than most of us to avoid living in a consumer culture that's without quality; he can afford at the very least to vacation in France.

Junk and margarine and McDonald's hamburgers are things I don't like, but I am not at all convinced that there is anything that can be done about them. I don't want to outlaw them (as Ralph Nader would outlaw my unsafe convertible) because I think people who want them should have them and because I doubt that there is much justification for outlawing even trash in a free society. Besides, I don't think Ralph Nader has the votes. He knows himself that he hasn't and often says that powerful people obstruct any reform. It is optimistic of him to persevere with his proposals for change anyway.

I enjoy being a consumer, and all I really ask of myself is that I learn as much as I can about who I'm doing business with and how I'm being taken, legally, every day. All of this interests me for its own sake. And I want to impart some of what I have been able to discover to people who would enjoy reading an amusing, opinionated book.

# 1
# backstage
## with betty crocker, ann pillsbury, and the jolly green giant

I remember as a child driving across the country and seeing for the first time the headquarters and factories of familiar corporations. It was a thrill and something of a shock to see what Procter & Gamble, Lever Brothers, and Dow Chemical looked like. I don't know what I had expected, but it wasn't what I saw in the ugly sprawl along the freeways. The only familiar things to me were the signs and company trademarks in front of the buildings.

Unless one happens to be in Minneapolis and takes the tour of the Betty Crocker kitchens, all he knows about the company that makes the Cheerios he eats for breakfast is what he has seen advertised, particularly on television. And the Betty Crocker kitchens provide only a glimpse into what goes on at General Mills, since they were designed to reinforce all the comfy feelings one has about Betty and Cheerios. There are no surprises in the pantry. General Mills, I am told, would have the kitchens even if there were no tourists. Products must be tested and recipes for Mrs. Crocker's cookbooks have to be proved. But the kitchens,

3

without tourists, would probably not look as they do—
like a stage set from a Doris Day film of the fifties. The
rest of General Mills headquarters is also gorgeous in
its fashion. What the visitor doesn't see is an entirely
different order of reality.

There are no tour groups traipsing through the central
offices of Pillsbury, also in Minneapolis, or through the
executive suite of Green Giant Company, the corn and
peas people in suburban Minneapolis. These two corporations, therefore, have not designed their offices as
showplaces. Pillsbury occupies several floors of an an-
cient downtown building, which could be the Travelers
Insurance Company or the Social Security Administration. Green Giant, whose activities and facilities are
dispersed throughout the country, has a newer headquarters, so tiny that the Jolly Green Giant would feel
cramped.

Slightly less than twice the size of Pillsbury in sales
($1 billion annually) and 116 on *Fortune*'s 1971 list of
America's 500 largest industrial corporations, General
Mills can afford magnificence. Behind Betty Crocker's
out-of-sight kitchens is a suite of offices embellished
with original works by famous artists—paintings by
Miro and sculpture by Henry Moore. Miro and Moore
are names in the elite art market but they mean little to
the Mass Market to which General Mills caters, which
is both foreign and familiar to General Mills' natty executives. *They* cultivate a square, circa 1945, image for
the company, but, as might be expected, they have no
use for it personally.

In life style, taste, temperament, and even food preferences General Mills men have nothing in common with

most of the people who buy their products. Some of them don't know Bisquick from library paste. When they eat cake in the executive dining room, they aren't necessarily eating General Mills cake, for this largest of the Minneapolis food companies contracts its own internal food service to an outside caterer. Imagine Henry H. Porter, Jr., the young Big G vice-president, who attended Yale and the Harvard Business School, who belongs to the Seattle Yacht Club and enjoys classical music, who speaks longingly of the way vegetables are cooked in French country restaurants, eating Bac*Os or Cocoa Puffs.

Porter says the General Mills executives don't always try new products before they are marketed, and if they did he wouldn't trust their judgment since they aren't at the level of a General Mills typical homemaker. Porter thinks he and others of his rank in the company like highly spiced foods and "taste levels too high to be acceptable with the general public." Testing out a new food product on a Big G executive would be, he says, "an absolute guarantee of disaster." The only way it might work would be to record the tastes of the executives and then go to work on products with alien properties. General Mills, in practice, tests products on consumer panels and relies heavily on their preferences. Without unlimited means, the consumers salivate over economy; without servants, they glory in convenience; without varieties of gastronomical experience, they delight in instant mashed potatoes.

General Mills does, however, allow for certain variations within the population in devising its goods. It fabricates cereals like Total for old people who regard vitamins as the next best thing to the fountain of youth. It sells Clackers (a graham cracker cereal) to the "nostalgia group," people who have fond childhood memories of graham crackers and milk. It sells sauces (some containing wine) to "the upper end of the Mass Market." Gourmets rarely use canned sauces. And the bulk of the Mass Market wouldn't know a good hollandaise from a Hohenzollern. Big G knows all this and aims for the market between the extremes.

Imagine H. Brewster Atwater, Jr., executive vice-president in charge of General Mills's consumer foods group, eating an instant macaroni main dish from a box. He gets no such fare at the Woodhill Country Club. But the Mass Market likes it just fine. Atwater recalls that General Mills made a Mexican macaroni which didn't sell well, but not because it was spicy, like real Mexican food—General Mills knows the Mass Market doesn't like hot spices. The problem was its name: the word "Mexican" has the wrong associations. The name was changed to Macaroni Montabello and that made everything all right.

Mercedes Bates, a General Mills vice-president, is at the head of a fifty-woman staff in the Betty Crocker kitchens. She came from *McCall's* magazine, and her taste runs to silver tea services. She is in charge of cookbooks aimed at millions—cookbooks that never call for sifting flour because housewives don't know, even when told, whether to sift first, then measure, or measure first, then sift; cookbooks that never call for unfamiliar ingredients or heavy spicing or fresh tomatoes when canned will do. Mrs. Crocker's cake mixes are developed in such a way that the cook gets a "satisfactory" cake even if she adds too much water or too little, whether she uses big eggs or small, and whether she cooks at too high a temperature or too low. The only way Mrs. Allthumbs can fail with a Crocker cake is to do *all* these things wrong. But then, sighs Miss Bates, "What can we do?"

No one at General Mills or Pillsbury will say that consumers wouldn't like cake mixes better if they tasted homemade—that is, made from scratch. Of course they would. But consumers, like the food companies, have other preferences as well—for economy and convenience, for instance. Consumers will buy the best quality food they can afford. A small percentage buys relatively expensive Sara Lee cakes from fresh eggs and fresh butter. The food industry provides the best products *it* can afford, while keeping a fixed eye on the profit picture. People think (as Big G wants them to think) that General Mills makes cake mixes, while what it and every other business makes is money.

The food companies, like other kinds of corporations, recognize that to maximize profits it is necessary to diversify. Pillsbury, General Mills, and Green Giant started out in the food field. That is what they know best and it has been profitable for them. The food business grows because there are more mouths every year. Still, population growth is not enough, and so the food people branch out into new ventures that are unrelated or only tenuously related to victuals.

The Green Giant Company is a dispersed operation with headquarters in LeSueur, Minnesota, executive offices in Minneapolis, and production in California, Washington, and Delaware. "Our twenty-fifth plant," says the company's chairman, Robert C. Cosgrove, "is the LeSueur Country Club which we subsidize to the tune of twenty-five thousand bucks a year. We don't tell our stockholders that openly, of course." The Le-Sueur Country Club is just one of many enterprises Green Giant has going which have little or nothing to do with corn or peas. Green Giant is also in the restaurant business, with Jolly Giant sandwich shops, full-service restaurants which the company hopes ultimately will be all over the country, and garden centers that exploit the Jolly Green Giant's green thumb to compete with Scott's Turfbuilder among the lawn-mower and fertilizer crowd. General Mills and Pillsbury are also going into diverting sidelines. General Mills, fittingly, makes Playdoh and Monopoly, as well as women's fashions and chemicals. Pillsbury owns the Burger King hamburger chain.

The Green Giant himself has not one but four advertised incarnations to promote the firm's varied interests. The first, no longer used, was a "Neanderthal right out of Grimm's Fairy Tales." In 1950 he was dumped in favor of the handsome blurry-faced Giant seen now on pea packages. When LeSueur peas were introduced to the snob trade, Green Giant created a spindly, gawky, hayseed Giant for use in New Yorker ads that needed that sophisticated touch. Now that Green Giant is in the fertilizer business, he has added muscle.

The company has changed as much as its famous giant since its founding in 1903, when a "Grade A" promoter named Silver Smith convinced sixty-seven LeSueur merchants that they should each put up one hundred dollars to open a cannery. Along the way the company's growth has been sustained through acquisitions of canneries; new crops (peas, mushrooms, snap beans); national advertising afforded by the company's development of a hybridized sweet corn (with three times the crop's normal yield); utilization of technological breakthroughs in frozen foods, boilable bags, and cryogenic freezing; and—of course—clever merchandising of the company's franchise, the Jolly Giant.

To reach a growth rate goal of 15 percent annually, Green Giant has found new businesses for which the Giant can serve appropriately as a symbol. He fits the garden center concept, and the garden centers give the company's seasonal employees something to do when they're not in the fields. The restaurants supply an outlet for food products (including corn-on-the-cob, frozen in the same way some people have their bodies frozen at death), and they cater to the eating-out trend. "If we don't go into restaurants, or food service of some sort, then we'll lose out because the volume sold through supermarkets is going down," says Austin Hayden, the Giant's director of new ideas for making money. "The vegetable thing is quite static."

General Mills has found comparable ways to pep up growth. Founded in 1928 by the consolidation of regional milling operations, General Mills was for some years the largest flour miller in the world. As it grew, Big G looked for other things to make "in search of enhanced margins and profit growth," says its chairman, James P. McFarland. Packaged cereals and Bisquick, cake mixes, and other products made General Mills "a major multi-line consumer food processor by the 1950s." The 1960s, however, brought diversification. "We began to look at ourselves," Mr. McFarland says, "not as manufacturers, not as food processors, but as a company whose basic strength and talent lay in the mass marketing of consumer products and services on which a brand position could be established." Thus, snack foods, crafts, games, toys, frozen foods, international business, and restaurants—and a growth since 1965 of 79 percent. Pillsbury, intensely involved in flour milling, has eased its distress over declining demand for flour primarily through its fast-food operation, Burger King, which operates in a market with rapid growth of about 14 percent a year.

Still, all three of these companies put most of their effort into food products, with which the companies are associated in the public mind and on which they will ultimately stand or fall. Their merchandising skills depend in large part on making consumers comfortable with their names and trademarks, which minimize the appearance of the massive, multimillion-dollar monoliths they are. To sell flour or green peas, a corporation must have a personality. Green Giant has the Jolly Giant to make its canned goods attractive on supermarket shelves, and the Giant is a sacred symbol. (Robert Cosgrove, who heads the company, was furious when Johnny Carson did a routine in Las Vegas spoofing his sponsors, including Green Giant. Carson made the giant out to be a homosexual. Did that upset Cosgrove? "Damn right it did. I've called Carson to task several times on it. You don't pay a guy to say things like that.") Apart from the Giant, Cosgrove has tried other, more conventional methods of transforming prosaic canned goods into something exciting to housewives. "We never had a 'Betty Crocker,'" Cosgrove says, "but we have a home services department. And we used James Beard about six years ago before he was really famous. We used him in two ways. One, we thought he'd be a good source for new product ideas. He was only fair. We'd take products down to him and he'd take them and add a pound of butter. More importantly we used him in conjunction with our home services department, at gatherings of home-ec gals. At this he was damn effective, because women would just hang on his every word, you know. He was a pretty good guy to have around, but we never could figure out how we could capitalize on him more."

Other companies personalize themselves with fictional female trademarks, such as Betty Crocker, Ann Pillsbury, Martha Logan, and Ann Page. None of them ever breathed a real breath, although there has been some confusion about that. Bob Barker and June Lockhart, the television personalities who preside over the annual Pillsbury Bake-Off, once pointed out to viewers a woman they said was Ann Pillsbury, but company officials say that that was a mistake. She is not the aging doyenne of the company or anything like that. An actress impersonated Betty Crocker in television commercials in the days when Cheerios sponsored the Lone Ranger, but Big G abandoned that years ago. Martha Logan symbolizes the products of Swift & Company; all Swift's dieticians are called Martha Logan. Ann Page is the brand name used by A&P (A&P, get it?) for its stores' private-label foods. Neither Martha Logan nor Ann Page ever became much of a personality. All the ladies were created to feminize large corporations run by men—as come-ons for their predominantly female clientele. Everyone seems to agree that in this sorority Betty Crocker stands out as a winning gimmick.

Mrs. Crocker (I assume she'd be married) has had at least five guises. Over the years artists for General Mills have done portraits of Crocker that represent the company's idealized vision of the typical woman. From time to time Crocker has changed, but she hasn't aged. One of the early Crockers looked regal and aloof. When it appeared that she wasn't with it she was turned into a more homey, less imposing Betty. All the Crockers, save one, had in common a rather styleless frumpiness. The latest, however, is a fashion plate, reflecting changes in General Mills' corporate structure. Since Big G acquired nonfood firms that made dresses, accessories, and such, it was felt that Betty Crocker should become a fashion-conscious lady. She now wears pearls, a dressy suit, and what looks like a silk ascot. No one, I'm told, posed for any of the Betty Crockers, including the latest sveltest one, so there is no chance anyone will ever run into her on the street. Betty is an ideal, Mrs. Composite America, and therefore doesn't look exactly like anybody. The fact, of course, doesn't prevent executives from acting as if she really existed. It's hard not to love a lady who has made such a bundle. Pillsbury, by contrast, definitely does not love Ann Pillsbury, because she never caught on with consumers.

Pillsbury's grain elevators stand parallel, across the Mississippi River from those of General Mills. And signs atop the buildings promote Pillsbury's Best and Gold Medal Flour, which compete in the declining United States flour market. General Mills has annual sales roughly twice those of Pillsbury.

Many Pillsbury products and advertising concepts are steals from Big G. In the fifties General Mills put out cake mixes that required the addition at home of fresh eggs. Market research had indicated that women felt superfluous if they made cakes from a mix that required nothing but water. General Mills thought they'd have more self-esteem if they had to crack the eggs themselves. Pillsbury, misreading the market, competed with mixes containing dry eggs. They were competitively priced, but sales were lower. They cost Pillsbury more to produce and, since women preferred General Mills' eggless cakes anyway, Pillsbury eventually came around.

Some years ago General Mills introduced an instantized flour called Wondra, processed (by agglomeration) so that it did not require sifting. Pillsbury answered with its own version of the flour. As it happened, neither product sold particularly well. Women liked the kneading texture of the old-fashioned flour they were used to and preferred the more satiny dough it produced. Sales, thus, were disappointing, but Wondra captured the bulk of what market there was, and it continues to make dough for Big G. Pillsbury discontinued its instant flour and now markets a variant of it. designed for special purposes such as gravy mixes, in which it retards lumping.

Ann Pillsbury, too, was an imitative response to Betty Crocker. But whereas Crocker serves as the trademark for a number of General Mills products, poor Ann has little to do these days, and company officials tire quickly of questions about her. One gets the feeling that they wish she would go away. She's been replaced by the Pillsbury Dough Boy, a relative of the late Speedy Alka-Seltzer.

General Mills clings to Betty Crocker as its link with the American housewife, and, in a funny way, she guards their door from attacks by the women's liberation movement, which has reason to be angry at General Mills. Until Mercedes Bates, the director of the Betty Crocker kitchens, became a vice-president of the corporation, there were no women in General Mills' top management. Mercedes Bates is still the only one, though she's barred by the nature of things from the executive washroom, the executive sauna, and the executive barbershop. She has a number of women in her department testing recipes, answering consumer letters, and writing cookbooks, but they are strictly incidental to a corporate hierarchy dominated by men. These men decide which products women are likely to buy and direct the company's women-oriented advertising. Miss Bates, a handsome lady without resemblance to any Betty Crocker, emphasizes proudly that her cookbooks sell in the millions and make a profit for General Mills. Male executives, out of earshot of Miss Bates, correct the impression: Her department is a drop in the ocean; she's for public relations, not profit.

A Betty Crocker is useful as an advertising symbol, but she's just the beginning of the merchandising process. The products on which her name and face appear have to be good. "Good" is a vague enough word to describe the complex of factors that goes into devising saleable products. They must, among other things, be economical, nicely packaged, easy to prepare or ready to eat, tasty, appealing in texture and appearance, and —last and least—nutritious.

Nutrition is a subject covered in elementary schools but forgotten by most adults. A number of people—

rich as well as poor—are said to suffer from malnutrition. Eating a lot is not the same as eating well if you disregard such things as the four basic food groups. It's assumed in the food business that consumers will not buy a product if it doesn't look and taste good, regardless of nutrition. People are said to be oblivious to anything advertised on the basis of nutrition alone. Trade associations, particularly the dairy and cereal industries, have tried to convince people that their goods are good for you. The Cereal Institute has promoted the notion that a balanced breakfast consists of fruit, *cereal,* milk, bread, and butter. The dairy industry says that, whether you like it or not, milk is nature's most nearly perfect food. Such appeals to the nutrition-minded may have some effect. But companies in the business of selling specific products firmly believe that to emphasize food value is not the way to sell anything.

Pillsbury, for example, developed and test-marketed in Chicago specially enriched flour and refrigerated biscuits under a contract with the United States Office of Economic Opportunity in Washington. The rationale for the study was that, since bread and flour are mainstays of poor people (who eat about three times as much grain food as upper income people do), a good way to combat malnutrition among the poor would be to put high-powered nutrients in bread. Pillsbury, in this case, added lysine, an amino acid which upgrades the protein in flour. The products were advertised as containing more protein per penny. But according to Pillsbury's report to the government, those who bought the products did so because they thought they would be noticeably different, not just more nutritious. Sales were only "moderately successful," according to Pillsbury vice-president Dudley Ruch. Profits weren't high enough to justify national marketing. "It was one of those god-awful gray-area things," says Ruch.

The key to selling nutrition is finding some other basis for advertising it. In other words, if wine is to be fortified with potassium to keep potassium-depleted winos alive to take another drink, at least it must be tasty wine. The cereal industry is keen on nutrition, possibly because it has often been criticized for making breakfast cereals with the food value of cardboard. Such enriched cereals as Total, Special K, and Product 19, particularly popular among older people, typify this industry interest. Dr. Ivy Celender, who heads the Nutrition Service Department of General Mills and considers herself General Mills' equivalent of Ralph Nader, tells how Big G goes about serving both the consumer's wants and his needs in the flour market. The covering of wheat is hard, brown, and rather indigestible, she says. American consumers don't like brown flour; "it isn't esthetically pleasing." But since nature has put many nutrients (B vitamins and iron) in the crust of wheat and since "nutrition is only as good as you can get into people," General Mills bleaches the flour and replaces lost nutrients with equivalent colorless synthetics. Dr. Celender says after all the subtractions and additions the nutritional value is the same.

Whenever possible, cereal manuracturers now try to fortify foods, whether customers care about nutrition or not. General Mills flour sold to restaurants, hospitals, and other institutions was enriched for the first time in September 1970. And to the extent that people do know and care about nutrition, the manufacturers cater to their concern. Dr. Celender says that surveys indicate people view protein as "good and desirable, something they want to increase." Carbohydrates and fats they think, are "undesirable and unhealthy." These assumptions are of course false; carbohydrates and fats in balanced amounts are essential to a proper diet. But with eighty million weight-watching, fat-and-carbohydrate haters in the country, the food companies feel it's necessary to cater to their prejudices. Food faddist nonsense, according to Dr. Celender, inevitably influences industry. For people with special health problems General Mills has developed bread mixes completely lacking in flour, milk, eggs, and salt. And they've engineered a cholesterol-free synthetic egg.

Industry concern for nutrition is said to be almost exclusively motivated by public spiritedness. But the industry realizes that the public is becoming increasingly conscious of nutrition (Robert Choate's attacks on the cereal industry and the public reaction to them shows that) and that several new trends in eating behavior will have to be met by corporate ingenuity. Dr. Howard E. Bauman, associate director of research for Pillsbury, thinks that "food in the future will have to be portable, quick, require no preparation, taste and look appealing, and be nutritious." Already many people don't eat three meals a day. Two is enough for them. And meals as such are passing out of fashion. Many of us are beginning to live on more or less continuous snacking. It's important, therefore, that snacks supply the nutrients of the foods they have replaced in our diets. Bauman says people who eat breakfast don't always eat conventional breakfasts. If people drink Coke for breakfast, as some studies attest, then it should contain Vitamin C. "We have a moral obligation; if we know how a product is being used, and something is lacking in it, we ought to add it if it's technically feasible."

A third trend arises from the population explosion and projected food shortages of the future. If meat should ever become scarce or prohibitively expensive, meat analogs composed of vegetable proteins may save the day. General Mills produces a spun protein product called Bontrae, from which can be made all manner of meats, vegetables, fruits, and nuts—all of them convincing, delicious, and wholesome, or so they say. Pillsbury's most interesting entry into the food analog contest is Space Food Sticks, the nutritious compact-energy food developed for the National Aeronautics and Space Administration's space program and now available in supermarkets. Space sticks come in four flavors. The glamor of the space program interests kids and nutrition appeals to mothers. The sticks contain everything man is known to need in his diet except variety. Ten to twelve of them a day and nothing else will sustain life, though you'd lose weight quickly and an active person would need to eat sixty-five sticks to get all the calories he needs. General Mills executives confide, for Pillsbury, that the Space Sticks sell well once, but that people don't like the way they taste and many never buy them again. Pillsbury executives won't disclose sales figures but say they are at satisfactory levels. The company's executives in Minneapolis keep boxes of Space Food on their desks to offer guests. Yummy.

Ironically, the problem of the future may be overnourishment. Vitamins A and D, to cite two examples, are harmful to health in excessive amounts. This worries Dr. Howard Bauman. "There can be a danger of over-fortification," he says, if "power races" develop between companies intent on outfortifying one another in their race for the consumer's dollar.

Nutrition may not be very useful as a selling gimmick, but preoccupation with nutrition and with new, economically sound processes and products drives the industry to innovate. The man at General Mills who is largely responsible for the company's forays into new foods is Dr. Arthur Odell. Odell has had a rich and varied career in tailoring technology to the needs of consumers. He was awarded the Legion of Merit by President Harry S Truman for his contributions to chemical and biological warfare research during World War II. He was a pioneer in the study of male and female sex hormones and the development of the contraceptive pill. In Mexico he worked for the Syntex Corporation and later started a competing firm, Productos Esteroides, in Mexico City. After he and his partners sold out to the G. D. Searle Company, the manufacturer of Enovid, he went to work for General Mills making soybeans into meatloaf. He is a member of the Institute of Food Technologists and the National Soybean Processors Association, director of special programs for General Mills, and vice-president of the Provesta Corporation, a joint General Mills–Phillips Petroleum Company "food-oriented" venture. What he does for Provesta he won't say, but the odds are it has something to do with making protein out of petrol.

Odell's talent for turning one thing into another comes in handy at General Mills, where the object of the game is turning grain into cash. Late in the fifties, according to Odell, there was "quite a fascination" with high protein bread. And there was a lot of talk about fabricating a bread which would be nutritionally equivalent to steak—"a slice of bread equal to a slice of steak or something as unachievable as that." The basis for the bread scheme, which General Mills conceived in partnership with the J. R. Short Milling Company of Chicago, was to add plant protein to bread mixes. The Short Company had done work converting soybeans into a pure, bland, white powder free of the bitterness and impurities characteristic of soybeans. It was hoped that the protein level of bread could be boosted from roughly 12 percent to about 50 percent. But, Odell says, the project failed because the new bread had the wrong "crumb characteristics" and the "loaf size wasn't just right. I think it was one of those flash-in-the-pan things," Odell recalls.

Anyway, General Mills and J. R. Short broke off their liaison in the early sixties. General Mills' share of the community property was a sheaf of processing patents for converting soybeans to new uses. The processes themselves had been developed by Robert Boyer, a protégé of Henry Ford who later went to work for Ralston Purina. Ford's "love affair with the soybean" made him think it would be possible to make auto bodies out of the stuff. Also he wanted to upholster his cars in fabrics made by spinning soy into a sort of artificial wool. "Wool," says Odell, "is protein that's been spun by sheep," so it wasn't really such a hair-brained idea.

Ford had already developed a successful soy-based ice cream, which Odell recalls didn't go over with the Food and Drug Administration "because it was too much like ice cream." But just as Ford and Robert Boyer were perfecting their process for spinning soy protein, synthetic fabrics like rayon and nylon came on the scene. They were superior in every way and thus pretty much killed the soy fabric business. Boyer, however, refused to be disheartened. He decided that if harsh chemical treatment of freshly spun soy protein did not result in a good textile, perhaps it would be good to eat. Maybe spun protein could be the basis for a new food system. The muscle fibrils of beef, chicken breasts, and other meats resembled soy in its spun form. To make facsimile meat of it, all that was needed was the addition of fats, coloring, and flavoring.

The idea didn't really take off until about 1957, because up to that time there was no commercial source of edible quality soy protein. Soybeans were widely used as animal feed, but their "microbiological level" was too high. In 1957, or thereabouts, Central Soya introduced edible quality soy powder which became instantly popular as an additive to sausage and in whipped toppings. In sausage it helped retain moisture and fat.

General Mills inherited the rights to the Boyer process and it had acquired Dr. Odell from the birth control pill business. Knowing "no more about protein than I knew about space travel," Odell went to work assembling a group of scientists who ultimately put in 350 man-years of multidisciplinary work on new products. The effort culminated in 1970 in the opening of a multimillion-dollar factory in Cedar Rapids, Iowa, from which General Mills began to unleash its soybeans on the world. General Mills markets Bac*Os, which are little bits of spun soy that look and taste like bacon. The basic ingredient of Bac*Os and the line of products being developed and manufactured in Cedar Rapids is Bontrae-brand tegretein, General Mills' version of spun protein. Big G and several companies (including Swift and Archer-Daniels) have written a standard of identity for spun soy, which they submitted to the Food and Drug Administration. A standard is a scientific description which establishes the definition and composition of the product. (There are standards, for example, for butter, margarine [imitation butter], and imitation margarine [imitation, imitation butter]. A standard functions to assure the consumer that the products are uniform and predictable.)

Bontrae has been engineered into a variety of ready-to-serve foods, including Bontrae Stroganoff, Bontrae à la King, and Bontrae croquettes. Restaurants in Albany, New York, have served it with great success. Odell has gone on to other, secret things. His contribution to General Mills has been in turning animal fodder, which is very cheap, into a human protein food, which is potentially less expensive from the consumer standpoint and also more profitable for industry than the genuine article. Bontrae, as it happens, can be made low in saturated fats (low cholesterol), high in vitamins, kosher, precooked, moist, free flowing, or flash frozen.

Food executives have a heavy burden to bear. Buffeted by the law, regulatory agencies, the press, and what consciences they have, they feel they cannot be dishonest. Pressured by stockholders and the profit motive, they feel they must turn a dollar. Schooled by the tastes of the Mass Market to some extent, they do not always know how far beyond these they can go in turning out either especially innovative or, on the other hand, cheaper and potentially inferior products. They don't really know what to think or to say about nutrition (enough? not enough? natural? synthetic?). They don't really know what they think about quality, since the profit motive so affects their decisions. Most of all, they don't know what to expect from the future. Trendwatchers in Minneapolis agree that they have a very unsure grasp of what people will want and will buy in the years ahead. General Mills' senior vice-president, Paul Parker, is afraid of the caprices of the marketplace and the constant possibility that predictions will fail. He remembers visiting the Curtis Publishing Company colossus several years ago and coming away with the feeling that it was an institution strong as Gibraltor. The decline of Curtis set Parker back on his heels and made him worry that the same sort of thing could happen to General Mills, if it does not keep abreast of consumer tastes and the exigencies of the marketplace. Neither he nor General Mills' vice-president and treasurer, Henry Porter, believes that it is possible to predict future tastes accurately. Porter says Big G used to think in terms of five-year plans; now it's two or three years ahead in its planning. He says he doesn't know what people will want three years from now. Whatever it is, he hopes General Mills will be making it. "Making it" is the abiding aim of the food industry.

# 2
# cashing in on cleanup

If the ecology movement follows the course of other popular crusades of the past decade—for civil rights and against war—it will fade away without having achieved its objectives of clean air and pure water. Attention spans are short, the obstacles are formidable, and ecology zealots haven't enough power to effect lasting, basic change.

The movement to "conserve what we have" and "to repair the damage already done" (Richard Nixon's phrases) requires radical measures that neither the President, Congress, nor the principal polluters in industry have been prepared to champion. Lasting change has little to do with returnable glass bottles or antilitter campaigns and nothing to do with the standard political rhetoric of ecology.

James Ridgeway in *The Politics of Ecology* refers to the movement that blossomed on Earth Day 1970 in the *past tense:* "Once the hysteria of the moment had passed, the politics of ecology seemed altogether dull, complicated and in the end paralyzing, bestowing on the participants a special sense of futility and alienation. It was an issue which told us only that we are all victims and that nothing changes." While Ridgeway's obituary is more prediction than history, there are grounds for his skepticism.

The basic technology for treating sewage and cleaning up water was developed in the nineteenth century but has never been used on a wide scale. Present sewage treatment plants and those that will be built (in insufficient number and with insufficient money) work well enough for human waste but not for the increasing tonnage of chemical industrial waste. Much of the money spent on these systems goes not into facilities but into the pockets of construction companies and consulting engineers who ask and receive excessive profits.

Setting standards for air and water pollution often occurs in secret meetings closed to the public, on the grounds that these discussions involve "trade secrets" of the offending corporations. And compliance with standards set in accordance with industry wishes is often voluntary; that is, there is no compliance. Companies with subsidiaries producing devices to control pollution are themselves among the principal polluters.

No one is against antipollution. But the control and ultimate elimination of pollution must, it is universally believed, take place simultaneously with the prospering of industry. Only if there is money to be made from pollution abatement, or if the public can be made to pay the costs, will corporations buy stock in the crusade. Nearly all the haggling that goes on in writing and enforcing antipollution legislation deals with the economics of ecology. Intelligent evaluation of measures proposed to limit pollution therefore requires the constant reiteration of the questions: Will it work? Who will pay for it? and Is the bill being sent to the right address?

About 85 percent of United States communities charge a fee for the use of sewers. Half of these charge additionally for handling industrial wastes. But in the Northeast, where industry proliferates, industrial user charges are rare. In Boston industry and individual residents pay the same rates, based on water use, though many industrial waste chemicals bollix up sewage systems with industrial indigestion. The output of filth by corporations is four times that by individuals. The general public pays a disproportionate share of the bill.

Former Interior Secretary Walter Hickel gave Edgar Speer, the president of U.S. Steel, a special clean-water award in recognition of his company's "initiative in pollution abatement" at two of its facilities. Later the government sued U.S. Steel as one of the biggest polluters in the country. Speer is known to feel that "ideal" pollution abatement programs are too expensive. "Unless the money for pollution control is intelligently spent—not by the dictates of emotion—the citizen is paying for something he didn't get," says Speer.

The chairman of Standard Oil of Indiana, John Swearingen, has taken this argument further. "The central question," he says, "is not whether we should have cleaner water, but how clean, at what cost. . . . Public enthusiasm for pollution control is matched by reluctance to pay even a modest share of the cost. This attitude will have to change."

Whose attitude will have to change? Effective pollution control legislation—the kind we don't have—would tell

Mr. Swearingen that if he makes a mess he'll have to clean it up at his own expense.

Making corporations liable for their own acts is difficult. After the oil spill off the coast of Santa Barbara in California the House and Senate passed liability amendments to the pollution laws—stiff ones, it is said. But though the federal law requires polluters to clean up oil spills, it does not make them responsibile to communities, businesses, or individuals injured by the spills.

James Ridgeway proposes that the government take on injunctive powers to force pollution abatement or close down polluting companies. He would regulate prices so that businesses could not pass costs on to consumers, and he'd pay for the cleanup out of industrial profits. Ridgeway, of course, would be the last person to think that the President, Congress, and the clean-water prize-winners in industry will endorse his proposal. That's why he past-tenses ecology.

For all of its resources and professed good intentions, Detroit says it won't be able to eliminate auto pollution as quickly as some politicians and ecologists would like. Late in 1970 Congress passed legislation providing for new, strict, nationwide standards—effective in 1975—for auto exhaust emissions. So there'll be a showdown as the effective date of the new law approaches and the car manufacturers appeal for extensions.

There have been a number of proposals, perhaps the most mischievous of which was Senator Gaylord Nelson's suggestion that, barring the development of a *clean* internal combustion engine, the internal combustion engine should be outlawed, and that a moratorium should be imposed on automotive styling changes, thus freeing industry money (about $1.5 billion a year) for developing a new power source for cars. In the pithy language of one of Nelson's aides, those recommendations "went right for the groin" of Detroit. Never serious, they were meant to illustrate what might have to be done eventually, if the automakers don't come up with satisfactory pollution control on their own.

Nelson's pollution solution got an immediate and predictable response from the heads of two major auto companies. William V. Luneberg, the president of American Motors, said he was "astonished." He "could only conclude that this senator has little or no knowledge of the facts of automobile design and manufacturing." Luneberg was not amused. Nor was Henry Ford II who, from Las Vegas, denounced "irresponsible demands and uninformed criticism." Changes in cars, Ford went on, "will not come one moment sooner because of deadlines which command the impossible." In other words, Congress can't require Ford to do what Ford is incapable of doing no matter how willing the company may be, and it isn't very willing.

As a serious matter, Nelson favored the enacted 1975 standards, which fix maximum emissions of the three major auto pollutants: .25 grams of hydrocarbons per mile; 4.7 grams of carbon monoxide; and .4 grams of oxides of nitrogen.

The uncontrolled internal combustion engine of the average car in 1965 emitted 11.2 grams of hydrocarbons,

73 grams of carbon monoxide, and 4 grams of oxides. The cars of 1970, better but not good, had cut emissions of hydrocarbons and carbon monoxide to 4.6 and 47 grams respectively. Oxide emission levels are higher than ever. The auto industry has a long way to go to meet the standards for 1975, which in effect would reduce auto pollution by 90 percent.

But is Henry Ford correct that it can't be done? Is the auto industry incapable of installing the desired improvements in time?

Detroit might meet the deadline by shifting to steam cars, cars powered by electric batteries, or some other power source, for which working prototype models already exist, but that isn't likely. All these, it is claimed, have serious drawbacks (appreciated best by the oil industry).

Wedded as it is to the internal combustion engine, Detroit doesn't want to fool around with anything "hairbrained." The pollution control of the future will likely depend on modifications of the existing internal combustion engine. And that's not easy to arrange.

However, what Goliath says it can't do has already been done by four Davids—students at Wayne State University in Detroit, who quite incidentally had daytime jobs at Ford. The car they entered in the 1970 Clean Air Car Race was a new Ford Capri, equipped with an exhaust gas recirculation system, electric fuel pump, insulated fuel lines, and a temperature-sensing carburetor. Using lead-free gasoline exclusively, the students drove their car thirty-six hundred miles from the Massachusetts Institute of Technology to Cal Tech. A requirement of the race was that the cars entered be able to maintain turnpike speeds. To win, a car had to perform well, be practical, relatively low in cost, capable of mass production, and low in pollutant emissions.

Senator Nelson took particular delight in the Wayne students' victory. Emission of pollutants from their car was well below the 1975 standards. Hydrocarbon emissions were down to .19 grams per mile (the federal standard calls for a maximum of .25). Carbon monoxide was down to 1.48 grams (the federal standard is 4.7). Oxides of nitrogen were reduced to .29 grams (the federal standard is .4).

Impossible, Mr. Ford? Astonishing, Mr. Luneberg?

Senator Nelson is as hard on his industry critics as they have been on him. "As Mr. Luneberg well knows," he says, "the entire automotive industry was engaged in an illegal conspiracy from 1953 to 1968 to delay the development and installation of air pollution control equipment on motor vehicles. . . . It seems obvious that the public is justified in having grave doubts about the sincerity of the automotive industry in its never taking significant action in dealing with the emissions from the internal combustion engine, which account for some sixty percent of the nation's air pollution problem and up to ninety percent in some metropolitan areas."

What about garbage? According to *Appliance Manufacturer* magazine, "There is money to be made by producing appliances to solve the garbage problem."

The Whirlpool Corporation is marketing nationally for the home a "Trash Masher" which flattens garbage in much the same way those big machines make art out of junked cars by squeezing them into solid metal blocks. In the case of Whirlpool's device, which is said to be "the first new major appliance since the household clothes dryer was introduced thirty years ago," a small motor powered by ordinary house current activates a ram that exerts two thousand pounds of force to reduce cans, boxes, bottles, and assorted scraps to about one-fourth of their original volume.

The product of this performance is not art; it's still garbage. And the performance is not show biz, although flattening aerosol cans may have the brief hold on the adult attention span that putting pennies on railroad tracks before the train passes once had for little boys. The home compactor is strictly functional, not frivolous, though it comes in three "decorator colors" and has "an attractive vinyl top like that found on most luxurious automobiles."

Look at what Trash Masher can do for you. Each time you have something you want to discard (provided it is not a personal hygiene item, a container of poisonous or highly flammable material that might leak out into the kitchen or catch fire under pressure, or a pressurized can that's not completely empty), you pull out the compactor drawer, throw in the refuse, turn a key, flip a switch, and sixty seconds later it's been flattened and deodorized. The deodorizing is taken care of by an aerosol spray released each time the drawer is closed. The spray can needs to be replaced periodically.

The effect of the flattening is that you have to empty the rubbish less often. The special compactor bags, which sell for about thirty-five cents apiece, hold twenty-five to thirty pounds of refuse, or about as much as you could put in an uncompacted state in three large garbage cans. The average family of four using a compactor would have to take out the trash only once a week and it wouldn't have to contend with unsightly garbage pails smelling up the house. The Trash Masher, in short, makes garbage fun.

In addition to the very few things you shouldn't under any circumstances put in a compactor, Whirlpool recommends that wet garbage continue to be separated from bottles, cans, cardboard, and such, and that the wet stuff go down the garbage disposal. (About 20 percent of U.S. households have garbage disposers.) Furthermore, care must be taken to prevent children from operating compactors, for though the machines have various safety features, they are by no means totally safe. A key is required to activate the compactor. After it's been turned and the switch has been thrown, the power ram descends. Should anyone try to open the drawer for some reason during the sixty-second compaction cycle, the machine shuts off. Despite these safeguards, the compactor will crush anything it will hold, including, perish the thought, small pets and infant children, not to mention diamond bracelets. A saleslady who demonstrated a compactor for me said one man told her he'd buy it if they had one large enough for his wife. The hazards are no joke.

Whirlpool and Sears Roebuck, which sells the Whirlpool compactor (for less money) under its own tradename Kenmore, have made much of the home compactor's contribution to the antipollution war, in which waste disposal is an important battle. We know that some 500,000 pounds of trash are created every minute, that each person is responsible, on the average, for 5.3 pounds of refuse per day, and that the U.S. Public Health Service expects that by 1980 the figure will be 8 pounds. Annually, Americans dispose of 48 billion cans, 26 billion bottles, and 30 million tons of paper.

Municipal incinerators are among the major air polluters, and landfills in many areas are about used up. Baltimore's two incinerators, for example, couldn't accommodate the entire 540,000 tons collected locally each year, so the city had to look for a private company to take on part of the job. This, potentially, is where the compactor comes in.

Atlanta, with the help of a federal grant, agreed to place four hundred Whirlpool compactors in selected homes for a test of new collection and disposal procedures. Atlanta's mayor said he expected that, for these residences, trash collection could be curtailed to once a week. Such an eventuality on a mass scale could reduce the cost of solid waste disposal, since collection is far more costly than the ultimate disposal.

But that's the hitch. As Sears admits in its promotional material, "the wide use of home compactors would be necessary before cities would realize . . . benefits." In all the years since garbage disposals came on the scene only a fraction of U.S. families has bought them. How many compactors does Whirlpool expect to sell? If projections exist, the company won't divulge them; they're trade secrets. It seems safe, however, to guess that only a relatively few, gadget-minded families will be able to afford a $250 garbage can such as the Trash Masher.

Even to those who can afford a compactor, it may seem more trouble than it's worth—finding space for it (rectangular dimensions: 34 inches high, 15 inches wide, 24 inches deep), stocking a supply of special bags and deodorizer spray, keeping the kids away, remembering what can't be compacted, paying the electric bill (said to be small), and keeping it in repair. What's more, once you have a compactor, you still don't have a complete home waste disposal system. Ideally you should use the sink-fit disposers for wet garbage and food scraps; the compactor for bottles, cans, and plastics; and a smokeless, odorless, indoor gas incinerator for combustible trash.

Which brings us to the garbage disposer, the second part of an "ideal" home waste disposal "system," and its contribution. Garbage disposers get food scraps out of house and out of mind but overload sewer systems. All new homes in Beverly Hills, California, are required, by ordinance, to have them. But New York City, the largest market in the country, bans them. Why? Because by taking the burden off the householder and a job away from the garbage man they overwhelm the sewers. *Appliance Manufacturer* magazine has reported that universal use of disposers would raise sewage costs 30 percent in one city studied. That's cheaper than carting garbage across town to some disposal point, but so what?—sewer systems across the country can't handle what's flushed into them already. Do garbage disposers "tighten the garbage gap," as *Appliance Manufacturer* puts it? No, but making people think they do can't hurt business.

To round out the home waste disposal system you will need a gas incinerator connected to a chimney in your kitchen. Then you won't have to take trash outdoors in the rain, if you ever did. The wonderful thing about the latest gas incinerators, which have not caught on with consumers, is that they are "smokeless and odorless" because they are equipped with afterburners that take out many of the pollutants from smoke. What the gas people mean by "nonpolluting" is that the newest incinerators are less polluting than trash fires used to be. They reduce smoke by 40 percent and carbon monoxide and nitrogen oxide emissions to a fraction of the amount in auto exhaust.

The gas industry, particularly the American Gas Association, is irritated that many officials and local ordinances are hostile to incineration and that in some cities people with incinerators have to pay fees for installation and regular inspection. Chicago is a particularly tough nut to crack for the gas industry because the city's Commissioner of Environmental Control, H. W. Poston, regards incinerators as polluters. Chicago "makes life difficult for the consumer," writes Arnold P. Consdorf, the associate editor of *Appliance Manufacturer.* He means Chicago discourages incinerator sales.

Poston claimed he wasn't anti-incinerator, merely against pollution, especially that from "old, poorly designed, and improperly operated models, that 'cook' garbage and put out a lot of particulate matter and odors" into the atmosphere. "There are incinerators on the market that can be approved," he says, "but you still have some problems, even with new apartment buildings using the latest equipment."

The American Gas Association tried to eliminate "the deterrent that . . . regulations provide to the potential buyer" by persuading the National Pollution Control

Administration to let the American Gas Association's Cleveland laboratories become the approving authority for gas incinerators. In other words, the industry that profits from the devices wanted to be in a position to judge whether they comply with antipollution laws—a conflict of interest if there ever was one.

Long-suffering ecologists see a patch of blue sky every so often, when big industry reacts to consumer pressure. One of the country's wealthiest corporations, Coca-Cola, committed itself at least verbally to the fight against pollution when company president J. Paul Austin announced an ad campaign promoting the returnable bottle with the slogan "Wouldn't you rather borrow our bottle than buy it?" And he reported that Coca-Cola has invested in Aqua-Chem, Inc., a firm developing sophisticated water purification systems. As a side venture, Coke bought two glass-grinding machines and installed them in an Atlanta supermarket; anyone disturbed by the proliferation of one-way glass bottles could bring back his empties and have them pulverized. There was no cash return for the consumer in this experiment, though some companies will pay one-half cent per bottle. The Coke bottles in Atlanta were ground into sand—not fine enough for the playground sandbox, said Austin, but good enough for industrial purposes.

Soft-drink companies have not been as pressed to innovate as have beer brewers and the makers of cans and bottles. Most soft drinks are made and packaged by independent industries, while beer companies usually brew, package, and distribute all themselves.

These industries are anxious to keep a clean public image—anxious enough to donate several millions of dollars yearly to "Keep America Beautiful." If Susan Spotless could only persuade people to keep bottles and cans out of sight, the theory runs, no one would care where the trash ends up. Can companies have taken an expensive step forward in their campaign to conceal litter. Hoping an agile half-step will obscure the mess, they have financed a recasting of metal dies to print this request on every container: "Please don't litter—dispose of properly."

But the consumer may not submit to motivation-planning quite as easily as corporations would like. Citizens of Bowie, Maryland, organized a lobby to outlaw one-way beverage containers in their town, and won. The city council ordered a ban on everything but returnable bottles with $100-a-day fines for stores that violate the law. Bowie was only the first of several towns considering action to cut down on wasteful packaging.

Can manufacturers are the most vulnerable to this sort of public action, and Reynolds Metals has organized a program to demonstrate its awareness of this fact. In cooperation with Coors Beer (of Golden, Colorado), Reynolds stepped up an experimental system to collect old aluminum drink cans at one-half cent each and use them for scrap. During the first half of 1970 Reynolds bought back over 16 million cans for eighty thousand dollars—respectable, but not nearly enough, since more than 24 *billion* drink cans are produced annually. And nobody wants the steel ones.

The polyvinyl chloride container is another embarrassment to the packaging industry. Pollution fighters complain that this plastic gives off corrosive chlorine gas when burned, destroying air-cleaning devices and harming nearby shrubs. They have tried to organize a nationwide boycott of articles in polyvinyl chloride bottles, but have run up against an identity crisis: there's another, harmless plastic that looks just like polyvinyl chloride. Until ecologists are certain that polyvinyl chloride is off the market, they recommend only soft-plastic and glass bottles.

The detergent industry has suffered worse publicity for its alleged contribution to algae buildups in public waters. Ecologists say detergents account for 50 to 70 percent of the phosphate in metropolitan sewers—supplying the essential nutrient for algae. Canada in 1970 decided to limit the phosphate content of detergents to 20 percent, a drastic reduction in some products. Since then, the soap companies have been arming for a difficult battle in this country. Spokesmen argue that no effective substitute for phosphate has been found and, furthermore, that carbon is the real cause of algae growth. The Soap and Detergent Association predicts that lowering the amount of phosphate in detergents will bring "significantly poorer cleaning levels, and a cutback in the nation's health, sanitation, and cleanliness standards." The only solution to water problems, they insist, is construction of complex new purification systems at public expense.

As if the public were not confused enough, Surgeon General Jesse Steinfeld in the fall of 1971 advised housewives against the use of nonphosphate detergents and recommended a return to the old, polluting phosphate products. The reason for the government's unexpected retreat: caustic soda, an ingredient in many of the new, nonpolluting detergents, is toxic and may cause death if ingested. Oddly, there was no suggestion that such dangerous chemicals be banned.

The enemies of phosphate are not deterred; they hope to convince the American housewife that clean water is more important than clean clothes. A mixture of soap and washing soda, they say, is the most ecologically safe detergent, but low-phosphate products are all right for the weak-hearted. They go by the Federal Water Quality Administration phosphate list in recommending Diaper Pure, Wisk, and Trend as the three least harmful.

Pesticides have long been the natural enemy of ecologists, and by now the list of dangerous chemicals is almost too long to remember. There is an easy way to recall the worst ones—their initials spell DEATH: Dieldrin, Endrin, Aldrin, Toxaphene, and Heptachlor. Antipollution groups put six others in the same category: DDT, Chlordane, Lindane, Mercury, Lead, and Arsenic. A small newcomer is Shell's "No-Pest Strip." The Department of Agriculture has warned that this insecticide should not be hung where old people, invalids, or infants are confined, and it should not be used where food is prepared. The warning is not a part of Shell's advertising.

All insecticides are poisons, and the consumer must usually decide whether he prefers bugs or chemicals. A "Do-It-Yourself Ecology" pamphlet distributed by Environmental Action of Washington, D.C., hints cryptically at an alternative solution. A helpful note says that "some birds, such as purple martins, eat up to 1000 mosquitoes a day." There is great potential for the gecko, too. He's a small, nocturnal lizard that thrives on cockroaches and other bugs; set him loose in the kitchen and you need never see him again. Ladybugs and praying mantises help kill garden pests, but no one has tried selling them on a large scale.

Many ecologists are convinced it is more effective to attack pollution at its industrial source than to organize boycotts. Court suits have been filed against oil companies for water pollution, against DDT users for destruction of wildlife, and against numerous factories for air pollution. Michigan has passed a law that widens the possibilities for civil suits against polluters. State residents no longer have to prove personal damage; they need only establish the polluter.

Based in Stony Brook, New York, the Environmental Defense Fund (EDF) has been waging a legal attack on pollution for several years. The organization, which calls itself "one anti-pollution device that works," collects dues from a national membership to finance a "limited number of carefully chosen" legal cases. Says the promotional pamphlet, "EDF will consider any kind of environmental case, and will tackle any offender— including the federal government."

With all these new outlets at his disposal, a well-organized pollution fighter need never be bored. When he is not building a case against the nearest industrial polluter, he can devote spare moments to selling aluminum cans, grinding bottles, boiling his clothes, and breeding purple martins.

# 3
# your neighborhood grocer

In periods of high unemployment and rising prices, consumer behavior may change. Women buy cheaper cuts of meat, more carefully compare prices among stores and brands, and take what they can afford rather than what they want. If shoppers are diligent and know math, they can economize. But they won't get much help from the food business, which prefers consumers to choose not on the basis of cost but because of the advertising, packaging, and sex appeal of products.

Despite the federal Truth in Packaging Law passed in 1966, groceries continue to be sold in odd sizes and at prices that confuse and are meant to confuse price-conscious housewives. Truth in Packaging requires that food processors tell how much of a product is in the box, but the law doesn't require whole or even numbers. Which is cheaper, a box containing $17\frac{3}{8}$ ounces and selling for sixty-one cents or one containing $11\frac{4}{5}$ ounces, selling for thirty-nine cents? The law doesn't discourage industry from in effect raising prices by reducing the contents of a package, while keeping the old familiar "price." This practice is known as packaging to price, and it affects hundreds of familiar items.

With eight thousand individual products to pick from in the average supermarket, who has the time, not to mention the mental agility, to shop with discrimination? Consumers Union, the nonprofit research organization, sponsored studies both before and after Truth in Packaging was adopted to see if well-educated, middle-class women could pick the least expensive brands and sizes in buying a basket of food. In both studies the women were wrong as often as they were right. Consumer experts have long believed that price comparisons would be easier if we had "unit pricing," that is, if supermarkets provided shelf tags showing not only the price but the cost per ounce or per pound, as is now required by New York City law for certain foods.

Where unit pricing has been tried experimentally, it has shown how dramatic savings can be. Safeway, the second largest food retailer, was the first to test unit pricing, at the suggestion of New York Congressman Benjamin Rosenthal. It works like this: A brand of instant "freeze-dried" coffee comes in three sizes—jars of two ounces, four ounces, and eight ounces. The shelf tag lists the prices of the three jars as $.65, $.99, and $1.85. In addition, it tells how much each jar of coffee costs per pound. The smallest is the least economical, selling for $5.20 per pound. The largest size, on the other hand, costs, on a per pound basis, $3.70. In this instance the shelf tag shows the truth of the common belief that for a single brand it pays to buy the largest size. Oddly enough, though, there are instances in which this is not the case. Comparisons be-

*tween* brands are possible too. Again, with exceptions, brand names are not the best buys.

During the Safeway experiment some of the chain's stores gave shoppers little slide rules for making their own computations. It was not successful; shoppers quickly lost interest. Both unit pricing and the slide rules aroused suspicion in black neighborhoods when they were first tested. Poor people can't always afford the larger, more economical sizes. Also, some shoppers thought that the pricing scheme was just another merchandising gimmick that in the end would cost rather than save them money. Some retailers say the skeptics are right. The calculations and shelf-labeling necessary for unit pricing may increase a store's overhead and ultimately get added to the consumer's food bill. One way or another, it seems, the food people will get theirs.

The supermarket industry claims it depends on satisfied customers for the repeat business that is necessary for profit. Selling spoiled meat, stale bread, and sour milk doesn't make sense, industry people say, because customers won't stand for it. Since store managers are only human, it *is* possible, now and then, that a loaf of moldy bread or a smelly, greenish steak gets sold. That's why reputable stores have guarantees.

But a different cast can be put on the facts. Supermarkets depend for profits on clearing the shelves of merchandise. Store managers get bonuses for high turnover and are docked when they have to throw away bad meat or return goods whose shelf life has elapsed. Unsold food is money lost, so it is to their advantage to sell everything. Therefore, grocers customarily put fresh merchandise behind the older stock on the shelves. And until open dating was introduced in some stores they kept the true age of foods a carefully guarded secret, so that customers couldn't discern freshness for themselves. Nearly all food products are coded in some way to show their shelf life, the date beyond which they are unsafe to eat, or the date they were packaged.

The number "606" on a carton of milk in one store, for instance, means that the milk should not be offered for sale after June 6. The code "5121" tells when a package of hamburger will likely be rotten. (Add the first and last digits to get the month; the middle digits represent the day. The expiration date on the ground meat is June 12.) The codes get complicated. The number "031" on pork chops in the store may indicate that they will be good until the first of the month and that they were packed at 3:00 P.M. May 30 on a carton of eggs reveals that they were packed on that date; their shelf life is seven days. A red mark on a loaf of bread means it was baked on a Monday or a Thursday, white means Tuesday or Friday, blue means Wednesday or Saturday. The code "6029" on bologna means it was processed by packer number 9 and that it should not be sold after June 2.

The codes vary from product to product and store to store, even within a chain, and grocers claim that even they sometimes don't know what the cryptic message means. In such cases manufacturers' or distributors' representatives come around to decipher the codes and, presumably, remove the old stuff from the premises.

The food industry has not wanted customers to understand the codes. Clarence Adamy, the president of the National Association of Food Chains, has said that if customers could read the codes they would "tend to buy only the freshest products" and that would create "monumental waste." If housewives got picky, Adamy said, there would be a substantial increase in cost, hence prices. Stores should be the sole judges of what is fresh enough to market, he feels, and customers should trust them to be responsible.

But there is little on which to base trust when codes are ignored and products offered for sale well beyond expiration dates. In 1970 former New York Congressman Leonard Farbstein and the District of Columbia Democratic Consumer Action Committee did a survey of eighteen stores belonging to three major chains operating in Washington (Safeway, Giant, and A&P). Some of the stores were in poor black neighborhoods, some in white suburbs and upper-middleclass areas. Ten products were monitored, including milk, eggs, bread, ground beef, and chicken. On the days the survey was conducted all but three of the stores were offering merchandise that was by their own standards too old to sell.

Ignoring code dates, one store manager said he discarded chickens only after they began to smell, "turn reddish or yellowish or when little growths began to appear." Another manager said that when a package of ground beef begins to look too old he "reworks it and repackages it." Only if it looks "too bad" does he throw it in the garbage. A third store manager told the survey team to leave his store. One market changed its bread code so that it indicated not the date it was stocked but a date two days hence. Another put too-old beef on sale at half price, while it sold equally anti-quated pork (cheaper meat thought to be bought more often by poor customers) at the full, original price. Lunch meat in one place was found to be two months past its "pull date." Some meat products were found recoded with new dates after original pull dates had passed.

Stores varied in what they considered the shelf life of some goods. Pork in one place had an anticipated life of two days. The same pork elsewhere was considered saleable for four days. Although conditions seemed worst in some of the slum stores, there were abuses in all but three of the surveyed supermarkets, in affluent and poor neighborhoods alike.

Many chains now employ "open dating," which can be read with understanding by customers as well as by supermarket cryptologists. But the industry as a whole is cool to the idea of truth in dating. It is cheaper to take back an occasional green steak when a customer complains than to be stuck with carloads of meat that's past its prime.

Four large chains dominate the market for food in the Washington, D.C., area—Safeway, Giant, Grand Union, and A&P. From time to time it's been suggested that the virtual monopoly these few retailers have in the nation's capital (they own 85 percent of the stores) is responsible for giving Washington the highest food prices in the country. There's little in the way of outside competition and plenty of opportunity for collusion in setting arbitrarily high prices.

Since Washington food stores serve, among other people, the families of congressmen and senators, Federal Trade Commissioners, Ralph Nader, the President and his consumer advisor, and hundreds of newspaper reporters, they are more closely watched and perhaps more rigorously criticized than those in other cities. And because of this scrutiny, they may seem worse than they are and actually be better than stores elsewhere.

When innovations are tried, they often are tried first in Washington. Safeway first experimented with unit pricing there. Cynics might conclude from this that the corporate grocers think if their behavior is exemplary and their practices progressive in Washington, where senators' wives shop, the government won't see any need to correct abuses.

In 1970 the Washington food chains began jiggering prices to woo customers away from each other and perhaps to disprove the common complaint that food costs had gotten out of hand. Where once competition seemed to be based on trading stamps and games, it was pegged to discount prices. The major supermarkets of Washington all became "discount" stores.

The discount fad which swept the country is worth a close look since it seems to contradict some of the things the big grocers had been saying about food prices. In 1966, when supermarket boycotts over high prices were staged in Denver and other cities, the major chains cried poverty. In New York, for example, one chain responded to boycotting housewives with signs in store windows saying, "Grand Union Earns Less Than 1½ Pennies on Each Dollar of Sales . . . Not Much Is It?"

This chain and others insisted that they could do nothing to lower prices, since they were barely getting by themselves. But by 1970 stores throughout the country were advertising reduced prices across the board (well, not exactly across the board; one lady wrote a Letter to the Editor pointing out that while one store advertised reduced prices on more than four thousand items, it also carried four thousand more items unreduced).

How is it possible for a small-profit industry to slash prices without eliminating profit and incurring the wrath of stockholders? Have things changed all that much since 1966?

The answer appears to be that prices, overall, were not reduced at all by "discounting," that in some cases they actually increased, and the food stores had never been as unprofitable as they said they were.

Safeway first "reduced" meat prices in its 221 Washington area stores by eliminating weekend sales and specials and by fixing "new low everyday meat prices." The effect was to penalize weekend shoppers and bargain hunters, since the new prices—while lower than the usual weekday level—were higher than the old sale prices. A Safeway spokesman said that projections were made which guaranteed that as much money would be taken in as before the reductions.

Some months later Safeway and the three other Washington monopolists extended discount prices to grocery items as well as meat. It is said that the idea behind this move was to lower prices and thus increase the volume of sales. Again, sales and weekend specials were eliminated or curtailed, and prices were averaged out so as to do minimal or no damage to profits. Had discounting been employed by only one or two chains, it would be easy to see how their volume might have increased; shoppers would flock to stores with lower prices. But all the big chains went discount, eliminating for the most part any distinction among them by price. It is conceivable that people were buying more food now that food was "cheaper" and that the added volume allowed for lower profit on individual items. But for Safeway, at least, a company official said he didn't know what the impact on profits was. He didn't know, or wouldn't say, by what percent prices on the average had been reduced. Too small a percentage to advertise?

The truth is, the food business, which is the largest merchandising industry in the country, is not as unprofitable as claimed. The best index of profits is not based on sales but on invested capital, which in the grocery business is relatively small. The National Commission on Food Marketing concluded in 1966 that store profits were generally higher than for other comparable industries and that grocers' returns on investment had never, in twenty years, been lower than for all industries. Supermarket profits (based on investment) run not to 1.5 percent but rather to a healthy 12.5 percent on the average.

Healthy profits might allow for real discounting, but it isn't likely that the new discount stores have decided that, as good citizens and inflation fighters, they should settle for lower profits. And it is even more unlikely that families noticed an appreciable difference in their food bills, which is the only meaningful test of discount pricing.

Discounting, like other magic merchandising schemes such as stamps and games, is a trick. I spoke to a grocery clerk who said that, when his store went discount, prices on some brand-name items were not lowered, they were raised. The store's private-label merchandise was reduced slightly. Shoppers comparing prices were made to think the discounts were greater than they really were.

By 1971 more than half of the chain grocery stores in the United States had converted to "discount pricing." Most major supermarkets had joined the trend— growing steadily since the early sixties—toward price competition in the retail food business. Oddly, as more chains went discount, the Labor Department's Retail Food Price Index climbed steadily, suggesting that the discount craze would, in the end, disappoint consumers.

Trade magazines admit as much in their discussions of how the trading stamp boom of the fifties gave way to the "merchandising of low prices," or rather the appearance of low prices. As *Chain Store Age* put it, it's "important to know . . . how the all-important *impression* [italics theirs] of low prices can be created and maintained."

In its April 1970 issue, *Progressive Grocer* inadvertently conceded that there is less to discounting than meets the eye, that there is nothing incompatible about the coexistence of discounting and rising prices: "The main theme of U.S. food retailing in 1969 was discounting, and it made a profound impact on sales, margins and profits . . ." (page 47); "Pretty much as anticipated, consumers were sometimes highly vocal in their reaction to steady increases in the price of many foods in 1969" (page 51).

Discounting is popular in periods of high inflation and unemployment, when consumers are especially price conscious. Like other selling ploys, it is transitory, useful from the retailer's viewpoint only for a while. As *Chain Store Age* puts it, "The rules of retailing apply: when the pendulum swings too far in one direction— too many stores doing the same thing, whatever it is —the situation is ripe for a new approach or a return to an old approach."

"Discount" is a word that is more often than not used to gull rather than to enlighten. A frequent concomitant of discounting is the elimination of expensive frills like trading stamps, for which customers pay as much as 2.5 percent of every sales dollar. When stores drop stamps, they can reduce prices accordingly without losing money.

The Washington, D.C., Democratic Central Committee surveyed Washington's discount supermarkets to determine what impact, if any, discount policies had had on prices. None, it concluded. The surveyors checked the prices of 113 items at local A&P stores, 75 at Safeway, and 94 at Giant, and found that more prices had increased or remained static than had gone down since discounting began. In A&P's case, 24 percent of the prices monitored were higher; 32 percent were lower and 44 percent the same. The results for the other two chains were similar and showed that, in the case of Safeway, while some of the stores' private-brand merchandise had declined in price, many brand-name items had increased. Spokesmen for the stores charged that the D.C. Democrats' sample was too small, their "methodology" all wrong. The president of Giant Foods, Joseph B. Danzansky, threatened that if the study adversely affected his stores' sales the consumer group would have themselves to thank for a rise in prices.

The *Washington Post,* with the help of two of the chains—Safeway and Giant—did a more exhaustive follow-up survey, which questioned the Democrats' findings. According to the *Post,* prices generally went down after discounting started—about 3 percent overall.

Reducing prices across the board is said to be possible because it increases sales volume. Shoppers switch to discount stores, or, if all the chains go discount as they did in Washington, consumers buy more because they can afford more. But it doesn't always work out that way.

At least one chain said that it expected from discounting a short-run drop in profits, one it could afford but probably wouldn't abide for long. Should profits not increase in a monopoly town where everyone had gone discount and where there was no distinction in prices to lure customers from one chain to another, the pendulum would swing in a new direction, perhaps back to bonus bingo.

A Coca-Cola ad on television or in a magazine tells the consumer that he should want Coke. A Coke ad in a trade publication like *Progressive Grocer* is slanted differently. It tells the supermarket manager how much money is in it for him; for example:

> Put a vending machine for Coca-Cola in your store. Up front. Near the entrance. It gives your customers a chance to start their shopping refreshed. And experience shows that shoppers who shop refreshed are in a more receptive mood to do their shopping and consequently spend more money. But why should it be a vending machine for Coke? Because you make a lot more money with Coke. In fact, if you've got six square feet available for a vending machine, you can make more than $100.00 a year per square foot by selling Coca-Cola.

What grabs retailers is dollars per foot of available space in their stores. Supermarkets are getting bigger. The largest have one hundred thousand square feet or more of sales floor. But with eight thousand items in the typical supermarket, the competition for shelf space is fierce. That's one reason brand names are drilled into our heads, so we will recognize them, ask for them when we go shopping, and thus force merchants to carry them.

The value of a company's franchise—that is, its name and trademarks—cannot be underestimated. It's crucial to company profits. In small convenience stores of the Seven-Eleven variety, which have limited space and carry only "top of the line" items, a company must have a name strong in the trade or it's dead.

Advertising in the trade press helps. An ad for Chap Stick lip balm tells grocers that Chap Stick is a "big impulse seller all year long." That is, people don't go into stores to buy it, but, if by some chance they see it next to the cash register, they'll take the bait. There is "more profit" in an eighteen-square-inch dispenser of Chap Stick than in "268 packs of gum. Or 107 cigar five-packs. Or 378 jars of baby food."

A division of Phillips 66 that makes ice cream containers points out that ice cream, like Chap Stick, is an impulse item. "A survey shows, out of 61 shoppers who pass the ice cream cabinet in a supermarket, 14 stop —and buy ice cream from it." Phillips 66 argues that if stores will only stock its distinctively shaped and colorful ice cream containers "it can help jump impulse buying to 18—or 20—or even more."

If the supermarket man is not motivated by the dollars-per-square-inch argument or the put-it-next-to-the-cash-register-and-it-will-sell-better argument or the our-package-is-prettier argument, perhaps he might snap up the free-trip-to-Hawaii-courtesy-of-Pillsbury offer. Eight grocers who go all out to push flour, cake, frosting, and refrigerated biscuits can take their wives (or guests) to the Pillsbury Bake-Off. (In 1971 it was in Honolulu.) One way to win is to write a personal letter based on sales success, beginning with "The Bake-Off worked for me because . . ."

Manufacturers wheedle some products onto the shelves by suggesting to the grocer that if he doesn't stock them he'll have to answer to his angry customers. Grocers were told to expect a run on fish sticks following the broadcast of a special program narrated by Glenn Ford. "As the first offering of the new TV season, 'America' will be attracting a load of attention . . .

22 million viewers in fact. And since 'America' is produced for and sponsored exclusively by Mrs. Paul's, those same 22 million people will be exposed to a dozen Mrs. Paul's commercials. High-impact commercials for our Onion Rings, Fish Sticks and Fish Fillets. . . . Your customers will be getting the Mrs. Paul's message loud and clear. And they'll be putting these Mrs. Paul's products on their shopping lists. Shouldn't you make sure your supply meets the demand?"

Luden's Extra Relief Cough Formula expects that between October and March (cold season) their television commercials are given 756 million "viewer impressions." In other words, we see them over and over and over again. The message is similar to Mrs. Paul's (bless her heart): "Stock Luden's . . . and keep your profits healthy."

The message is that supermarkets should not be out of stock when the hordes come rushing through the door. Gillette Soft & Dri is the "third largest selling anti-perspirant in America," and with "10 million free samples, 16 million cents-off coupons, 5 million dollars in advertising, no wonder you're out of stock." "Pream is growing faster than anybody else in the powdered creamer market. In just six months, we've doubled our sales. . . . How'd we do it? Our new 20 ounce jar is a big factor. Along with the heaviest advertising schedule ever. . . . (The 20 ounce jar gives you more profit per jar than any other national brand.)" "Health and beauty aids are one of your most profitable product categories. And Contac (cold pills) are the fastest selling health and beauty aid in food stores." Health *and* beauty?

Advertising in the trade press is of a crasser sort than most people generally see because it deals almost exclusively with the subject Commercial America cares about—profits. If the ads get into the wrong hands, they conjure up many interesting questions. For example, who pays for all those millions of dollars in television commercials, coupons, free samples, pretty packages, trips, and such? Could it be the consuming public? Are we really as gullible as they think we are, ready to grab on impulse whatever happens to be sitting next to the check-out stand?

The products we see in the stores are not, as we may have thought, just there. They are stocked for reasons far more complex than just because the consumers want and need them and because big companies make them. They are there because the middlemen in the supermarket business, like the rest of us, are targets of expensive advertising—advertising of a special sort which tells them that, sure as tomorrow, we will be in the stores craving fish sticks and antiperspirant. Because of advertising. And what advertising!

The Campbell Soup Company got into hot water with the Federal Trade Commission several years ago for putting marbles in the bottom of bowls of soup photographed for television commercials. The marbles forced the solid ingredients to the top of the bowl, giving the chicken soup a more chickeny look. The Federal Trade Commission thought that was a deceptive practice and Campbell altered its advertising.

The watery soup problem, however, remained. Canned soup is an economy item. And Campbell could not hope to hold down prices and at the same time put a lot of expensive meat in its soups. As an illustration of Campbell's concern for economy, let me cite a letter from William C. Parker, the company's director of public information. Mr. Parker objected to a price comparison I had made (in an article on unit pricing) between Campbell's chicken broth and chicken broth made by Banquet, one of Campbell's competitors. I had priced the two soups in a local supermarket and afterwards wrote that "Chicken broth was available in 14.5 ounce cans (Banquet) at two cans for 35 cents or in 10.5 ounce cans (Campbell's) at two for 33 cents. . . . Campbell's chicken broth cost six cents per pint more."

Now there's nothing that upsets a businessman more than the suggestion that his competitor's product is better or cheaper, especially when it isn't true. I had been careful with my arithmetic in making the price comparison, but I had neglected one very important fact which Mr. Parker brought to my attention in his letter:

> Campbell's chicken broth is condensed. That is, it is made double strength with no dilution, and the housewife is supposed to add a can of water to it at home. Conversely, the chicken broth with the Banquet label is 'ready-to-serve'—that is, the housewife does not add any water to it. Therefore, the housewife may be getting two cans (total of 29 ounces) of Banquet for 36 cents, but her two cans of Campbell's chicken broth (total of 21 ounces) for 33 cents will actually make 42 ounces of broth when it is prepared at home. She is getting a good deal more for her money from Campbell's chicken broth.

Mr. Parker went on, "Most housewives in America have been using Campbell's condensed soups for more than seventy years and are well aware that they are double strength soups and that the housewife is not having to pay the cost for having water shipped around the country, as she does when she buys ready-to-serve soups." It's said there's many a slip twixt the cup and the lip, and I was glad to know and make amends for the fact that my price figures, quite unintentionally, had been as deceptive as Campbell's marbles.

But Mr. Parker in his reference to "shipping water around the country" clearly was not anticipating the introduction of Campbell's latest soup product, Chunky Soups, the company's first entry in the ready-to-serve soup sweepstakes. Chunky Soups solve the marble problem. They are so thick—that is, so laden with meat, vegetables, and starch—that you almost can eat them with a fork. The ads say that. The Chunky Beef Soup I tried closely resembles in taste and appearance canned beef stew (never one of my favorites).

Unfortunately for Mr. Parker's pricing argument, Campbell's Chunky Soups dispense not only with the marbles, the costly shipping of water around the country, and the housewife's reputed preference for condensed soups but also with economy, and unabashedly so. Cans of Chunky Soup go for the hefty price of fifty-seven cents in the market I checked. I gather they are worth every penny of it. Campbell certainly thinks so, for its advertisements say, "you probably never paid this much for soup before, but then you've never tasted soup like this." I'll buy that, but not the soup.

Ralph Nader and other consumer defenders think they know what consumers *need.* Industry thinks it knows what they *want*—for example, Chunky Soups. Those who have studied Truth in Packaging and support the spirit of it talk a lot about package shapes and sizes. We all agree that in an ideal world packages would not contain less product than they seem to. They would come in a minimal variety of uniform sizes and in whole, even-numbered ounces or pounds that make it simple for the vaguest shopper to compute the cost of what he is buying and to compare brands. And they would list prominently the ingredients they contain. The 1966 Truth in Packaging Law does not require all of these "ideal" conditions, and it can thus be criticized for falsely advertising itself to a public prone to think that truth in packaging means exactly that. There are, however, people in the food industry who think *everyone* is better off because the law is imperfect. And while Congress thinks we *need* truth in packaging, there is evidence that we don't necessarily *want* it.

Take the matter of package contents. For years Bisquick, a mix for making biscuits and many other things, sold very well for General Mills. It had what was considered a "mature market," which is to say it was a proven product with substantial sales and relatively low costs to the company. People liked it and bought it, and it didn't require excessive advertising. Mysteriously, however, sales dropped off, and the product was in trouble. The makers of Bisquick did some market research to find out what the trouble was. They found that Bisquick was no longer being used to make biscuits. Why? People were buying refrigerated biscuits or watching their weight and eating less bread stuffs. They had found, however, uses for Bisquick other than the making of biscuits. But the formulation of Bisquick did not work as well for the sundry other uses as it did for biscuits. The study caused General Mills to devise a new Bisquick formula especially for these uses. The result was "New, Improved Bisquick" and a boost in sales. But whereas some people had complained about *old* Bisquick, now a substantial number of people were carping about *new* Bisquick; they liked it better the way it had been.

An easy solution would seem to be for the manufacturer to put out two versions of the product and thereby satisfy everybody. But that solution was considered unfeasible because, if it were tried, General Mills would be criticized for "undue proliferation in the marketplace." Consumer activists don't like unnecessary variety; it confuses people. Stores don't either, because they must already cope with thousands of different products, and there isn't shelf space for excessive variety.

As noted earlier, those who make it their business to give housewives shopping tips often recommend buying the larger sizes, which are nearly always cheaper. A sixteen-ounce can contains more for the money than, say, a twelve-ounce can. Canners, however, have noticed an odd phenomenon. Housewives don't *want* large cans. If they want a snack, they don't need a two-pound can of whatever it is they're eating. They don't want to eat a little bit, then leave the rest to spoil in the open can. The Green Giant Company, which dominates the market in corn and peas, has put out a variety of can sizes. And the merchandising lesson it has learned is that as can size is reduced, sales go up. The per-ounce cost of canned corn also goes up as the can size goes down. But according to Green Giant, housewives like small cans and they are more than willing to pay relatively more money to get them. Profits on twelve-ounce cans are twice those on sixteen-ounce cans; profits on eight-ounce cans, twice those of twelve-ounce cans. Hunt Foods extended the logic to absurd extremes by producing a five-ounce can and marketing puddings and diced peaches in four-packs of easy-to-open mini-cans.

It is no exaggeration to say that the five-ounce can revolutionized canning. Hunt's booming sales are the envy of the industry, and imitators have sprung up to capitalize on the mini-can. Brown-baggers now take little cans of peaches and puddings to work or to school for lunch. It does not matter that they are paying a premium for convenience and supporting proliferation in the marketplace.

Consumer protectors sanctimoniously believe that their efforts improve the quality of life, but they may in some cases diminish it. Green Giant, to cite an example, is obsessed with the quality of its products and continually strives to upgrade them—by breeding its own seeds, picking vegetables when they reach their flavor peak (sometimes in the middle of the night), and flying samples of every batch of vegetables to LeSueur, Minnesota, where tasters grade them for quality. The result of expensive quality controls is a product relatively more expensive than some other brands, particularly store-brand vegetables. Consumer protectors harp on the brand-name hoax and recommend that people buy unadvertised off-brands to save money. In many cases that's good advice, but Green Giant executives insist that all you need to do to find out whose peas are best is to compare the products; Green Giant's are best.

I've not been bribed to say that their self-interested claims are true, but they may be; who knows? Robert Cosgrove, the company's chairman, bragged to me that their boil-in-a-bag vegetables with butter sauce sold better than Birds Eye's comparable product because their butter was melted into the product at the processing plant, whereas Birds Eye's wasn't. People were thus able to look at the little butter pat in a Birds Eye vegetable and conclude for themselves whether the additional cost of the product was worth the little bit of butter that came with it. It wasn't. The inflated cost of Green Giant's peas in butter sauce was harder to detect.

The "needs vs. wants issue" is further illuminated by the packaging Green Giant uses in its frozen vegetables—the boilable bag. The cost of vegetables that come in boilable bags is literally twice that of frozen vegetables one must heat in a saucepan. Consumer protectors might say that that's a scandalous waste of people's money. The products nevertheless sell extraordinarily well, and no one should be so foolish as to claim that shoppers don't realize they cost more. They sell well because they are convenient. It is easier to drop a plastic bag of vegetables in boiling water and serve them sixteen minutes later than it is to heat vegetables in a saucepan, standing over them to make sure they don't burn, overcook, or evaporate.

# 4
# tenants' plight

It is said that 70 million Americans are tenants. (The 1970 census lists 23,554,976 rented dwellings.) And in most places, with laws favoring landlords, tenants have little to say about how they live, what they pay, or even whether they'll be allowed to continue to live in their rented homes. Although the Department of Housing and Urban Development claims that the traditional legal discrimination against persons who rent is disappearing—several states have changed laws, and tenants are winning suits against landlords in some places—the tenant's lot is still not good. This applies not only to poor people living in slum properties infested with rats and in chronic disrepair. Tenants in $800-a-month New York apartments have legitimate maintenance complaints. A tenant's primary uncontested right is to pay his rent on time. His responsibilities, on the other hand, are minutely detailed in the six-point type of the standard four-page lease he signs when he contracts for a place to live. .

There is an air of unreality about form leases. They are written in legal language that's difficult to understand in a quick reading in an apartment rental office. They contain provisions that no one could live up to. Generally, when the landlord is a corporation, the prospective tenant can't haggle over any of the terms of the lease (the lease stipulates that). And the landlord's agent or resident manager is not authorized to waive anything or make oral or written agreements that would in any way alter the lease (the lease says that too). The signing, then, is a required formality about which the new tenant must inevitably feel a certain halfheartedness. But whether he likes it or not, there is no alternative in a tight housing market in which landlords in general require similar leases. There is no comfort in knowing that, however fantastic its provisions, a lease is a binding contract.

So people find themselves agreeing that they won't let their children play on the lawn, throw cigarette butts in the toilet, watch television after eleven o'clock, drive nails in the wall to hang pictures, barbecue on the balcony, put flowers on the windowsill (inside or outside), or wash the car in the parking lot. They agree to carpet the landlord's floors, so as to protect tenants below from noise because the building is poorly insulated. They agree to let the management barge in to inspect their apartment at any "reasonable" hour. They agree not to "circulate to other tenants any type of literature, papers, circulars, periodicals or other such printed matter" without the landlord's "prior written approval." They agree in advance to abide by any rules or regulations the landlord might later choose to impose.

The lease I've been paraphrasing is one signed by tenants in a new and expensive apartment "community" in Montgomery County, Maryland, adjacent to Washington D.C. It is a legal contract enforceable in all its particulars at the whim of the landlord and at considerable potential expense to the tenant found in violation of its provisions. The vindictive landlord, having all the cards, can spot a lease violation just about anywhere he chooses to look for one (who *hasn't* hung a picture on the wall or watched the Dick Cavett Show?). And if nothing else occurs to him as a pretext, he can have the tenant evicted for "objectionable conduct," left undefined and "determined solely by the landlord."

When the landlord goes to court charging breach of lease by the tenant, the tenant has already agreed (in his lease) to pay the landlord's attorney fees and court costs, not to mention rent for the duration of the lease (up to a year) or two months' rent in "damages" to the landlord at the option of the landlord. The tenant also forfeits the one-hundred-dollar security deposit he left with the landlord when he signed the lease and on which he has earned not a cent of interest. The cost of losing one's home in Montgomery County could easily run into several hundred dollars.

The landlord has his responsibilities and liabilities too, but they are limited. If the building burns down, and the tenant didn't set the fire, the landlord has to put him up somewhere or free him from the lease. The landlord agrees to provide heat and airconditioning and hot and cold water, but he doesn't warrant that they will work properly, and he and the tenant agree (in the lease) that the landlord can't be held responsible for damages if repairs aren't made. If the tenant drowns in the swimming pool or his property is lost or damaged as the result of the landlord's negligence, the lease says it's the tenant's tough luck; the landlord has no liability.

Montgomery County, one of the four or five most affluent counties in the nation, is a bedroom suburb for many people with jobs in Washington. Apart from its wealth, it is typically suburban, having many single-family houses, many new high-rise and garden apartments, and in the Rockville, East Silver Spring, and Takoma Park sections some low-cost housing. Its landlord-tenant relations are approximated throughout the country. In contrast to Washington, where the courts have worked many progressive changes in laws affecting tenants and landlords, Montgomery County and indeed the state of Maryland is a bad place to be a tenant.

In a famous Washington, D.C., case several years ago a woman named Edwards, who was a month-to-month tenant in an apartment building owned by a man named Habib, complained to the city about a number of violations of the city's sanitary code which her landlord had failed to correct. The landlord learned of her complaint and gave her thirty days' notice to get out. Retaliatory evictions were legal in Washington, inasmuch as after a lease had expired a landlord could ask a tenant to vacate by giving thirty days' notice. Mrs. Edwards sued Mr. Habib and won on appeal. Retaliatory evictions are now illegal in Washington. Montgomery County has a strong health code, enforced by its environmental health department, but when a tenant calls in to complain about a landlord's violation, the caller is told that his complaint cannot be guaranteed confidentiality. The landlord may find out who reported him and in that event have the offending tenant evicted. According to the county attorney's office, "It happens quite frequently and it's perfectly legal."

In another important Washington, D.C., case tenants in a slum apartment called Clifton Terrace stopped paying their rent in protest of unconscionable living conditions. After eviction proceedings had been undertaken against them they offered to document for the court some fifteen hundred uncorrected violations of Washington housing regulations in Clifton Terrace. In that case the U.S. Court of Appeals for the District of Columbia ruled that "the tenant's obligation to pay rent is dependent upon the landlord's performance of his obligations, including his warranty to maintain the premises in habitable condition." In Maryland and in other states a tenant's obligation to pay rent is considered independent of the landlord's responsibilities. And there is no warranty of habitability. Withholding rent cannot be used as a lever to force the landlord to make repairs because the landlord can make an eviction stick.

Montgomery County attorney Phillip Tierney—in the middle of a battle between about a thousand members of the Montgomery County Tenants Organization and the local corporate landlords and their lawyers—was involved in drafting a proposed landlord-tenant code for the county. Tierney says the property owners argued to him that the leases tenants have to sign are justifiable on the grounds that owners need to protect their investment against transient and irresponsible renters who don't take care of their apartments and who leave after the lease expires. The landlords thought that no new law was needed and that, in any case, such legislation was beyond the scope of county government and should be a matter for the state. The real estate interests, Tierney adds, "have an effective lobby in Annapolis so they advocate state action knowing damn well any bill will be defeated there."

Tierney says county residents complained about retaliatory evictions and about precipitous rent increases after leases expired. During periods of high vacancy rates it is common for apartments to advertise cheap "below-the-market" rents in order to attract tenants. But after a tenant has been in the apartment a year, rents are adjusted upward by 25 or even 50 percent. People who have made improvements and want to stay where they are have no recourse but to pay. By contrast, in 1969 the residents of the luxury apartments Tiber Island and Carrollsburg Square in Washington were informed of rent increases running in some cases to 32 percent. Four hundred and fifty tenants balked, incorporated themselves as a tenants' organization, hired a lawyer, and began withholding from their rent payments an amount equal to the rent increase. The money was held in escrow pending the settlement of suits filed against the management company, Frederick W. Berens, by the tenants and against the tenants by the management. The escrow account accumulated thirty-one thousand dollars by the time a settlement was reached, under which all of the escrow money was returned to the tenants and the company agreed to limited and reasonable rent increases spread out over two years.

In low-rent apartments in Montgomery County, Tierney says, some notorious landlords, who do not offer tenants leases of any sort, run their enterprises "like feudal lords." One landlord walked about his property brandishing a gun at tenants. He made all sorts of demands, set arbitrary penalties for late rent, imposed fines for conduct he didn't like; he even set an eleven o'clock curfew for tenants to be in their apartments.

The Fair Landlord-Tenant Relations code proposed for Montgomery County was a modest attempt to give tenants leverage they had not had. It set up a commission to hear and negotiate disputes between landlords and tenants, provided for licensing of rental facilities to ensure that they satisfied certain minimum health and building code standards, empowered the new commission to establish rent guidelines pegged to the cost of living or some other index, and required lease standards (clauses that must be in leases and others that can no longer be included). Leases, for example, would be renewable at the tenant's, not the landlord's, option. Landlords could not terminate a lease without notice or without adequate grounds; leases could not free landlords of responsibility for negligent acts; leases had to acknowledge the landlord's responsibility to make repairs and maintain premises in a habitable condition; retaliatory evictions were prohibited; and tenants could not be made to pay landlords' court costs. The code was similar in many respects to the model law produced in 1969 by a research project of the American Bar Foundation under an Office of Economic Opportunity grant. The model law was intended to do away with what one of its authors, Philip Hablutzel, called "an archaic jumble of common law rules" ill-suited to modern urban society. The Montgomery County bill is not given much of a chance. The real estate interests are against it, and even if passed by the council, it could be vetoed by the county executive, whose enthusiasm for it is limited.

Increasingly, tenants throughout the country are becoming activists, forming tenants' organizations, suing in the courts, organizing rent strikes, and picketing. The movement was begun by poor people and by legal services (War on Poverty) lawyers in their behalf, but in the course of things a lot of middleclass people have learned that, as tenants, they have a unity of interest with the exploited poor.

The tenants' movement has involved rent strikes by students in Berkeley and Ann Arbor, suits by residents of luxury apartments in New York, and tenant actions in Chicago, New York, Cleveland, Detroit, and Washington. Some thirty-eight bills relating to tenants and landlords were introduced in the California legislature in 1970 (six of them passed). A habitability law was passed in Maine in 1971, and many states and localities have pondered changes in their laws (including Maryland's Prince Georges County, where 43 percent of the housing units are apartments). The National Tenants Organization, with headquarters in Washington, has two hundred and fifty affiliates in thirty-three states.

Although landlords predictably react to tenant militancy with hostility, there has been an effort in the industry to affect an attitude of conciliation toward unhappy tenants and actively to encourage tenants' organizations or, better yet, take them over. This blend of hostility and conciliation is evident particularly in the trade press. In one breath *Professional Builder* ("the business magazine of housing and light construction") equates tenant militancy with "rioting in the streets, Vietnam protests, the hippie and youth revolts" and says, "It is obvious that the tenant rebellion must be stopped. . . . It is a very real threat to the private housing industry." In the next breath *Professional Builder* talks up "better communication" with tenants, "a consistent goodwill program," ridding landlords of their "image of a faceless enemy," encouraging tenant associations, and enlisting their support "in common problems." *Professional Builder* specifically recommends revising leases to be "fair to both tenant and landlord." With the National Tenants Organization adding chapters all over the country, with the courts finding in favor of tenants, and with states changing their laws, *Professional Builder* believes in joining the movement lest it get out of control. What it seeks to prevent above all is rent controls ("the most dangerous and harmful effect of the new housing crisis") and the enactment of laws swallowing whole the American Bar Foundation's model tenant-landlord code, some provisions of which, says *Professional Builder,* "would surely make any landlord gag."

Lloyd D. Hanford, Jr., a San Francisco management consultant, writing in *Property Management* in its March/April 1971 issue, said, "whether or not local laws forbid retaliatory eviction, sophisticated management should absolutely refrain from the practice because it *not only may become the catalyst of a tenant mass action but also represent prejudicial treatment. . . .*" (Italics mine.) The tenant movement can thank itself for this new, enlightened self-interest in the housing industry, to the extent that such an attitude exists.

# 5
# television, on and off

The bulk of Saturday morning television advertising aims at getting children to persuade parents to buy things—toys (some of them hazardous), candy (bad for teeth), and food (snacks and cereals). Parents hounded by little kids may find such commercials distasteful. They are not, however, the Major Menace some consumer protectors think they are; and they do not, it seems to me, deserve to be regulated (or banned) in the manner of cigarette commercials. It is fair to expect that even in the absence of television advertising, children will eat candy and lust for cupcakes. If parents want it otherwise, it is they, not Congress, who are in the best position to lay down the law.

Robert Choate, known for his publicized attack on breakfast cereals ("empty calories"), is chairman of a group called the Council on Children, Media and Merchandising. Early in 1971 he issued what is called "a public appeal to the private food industry, advertising agencies, and the broadcasters of the United States" to adopt a "code for advertising edibles to children," and he urged the public to write to senators, to the American Advertising Federation, and to Choate's own group expressing support for the code. Choate wanted his recommendations adopted by "both industry and government."

Choate's code, among other things, would require that food advertisers publish the "true ingredients" and "major nutrients" in their products. In all but ten-second commercials, food ads would have to state the nutritional contribution a product makes and the role it plays in a balanced diet. Mention of specific nutrients would be permissible only when a food contains more than 10 percent of the Recommended Daily Allowance of the nutrient in question. (In other words, for Kellogg to advertise that its cornflakes are fortified with, say, vitamin C, the cereal would have to contain enough vitamin C so that ten bowls of cornflakes would provide all the vitamin C one should have in a day.) Advertisers could not claim their products in any way superior to other very similar or identical products made by other companies. When sugar or sweetness is used as a selling point, there would have to be an accompanying warning about tooth decay. No advertisement could offer a prize or a premium that doesn't make "a positive contribution to the child's improved physical health." No hour of children's television could contain more than four food advertisements. No drugs or vitamins could be advertised between seven and ten o'clock in the morning or between two and nine in the evening, or between seven and nine on weekend and holiday mornings. A cartoon or other character in a children's program could not be used to advertise a product. Sponsors, ad agencies, and broadcasters would be required to finance a study of the impact of television on children.

Robert Choate's intentions and some of his proposals are admirable. Yet the code he proposed is not. A number of substantial studies and reports have found that malnutrition is a problem among all ages and classes within the population—not merely the poor or the young—and that greater attention should be paid to the nutritional value of food. Only about one-third of us, it is said, eat a proper breakfast. And according to food industry sources, runaway sales in the snack food industry—crackers, cookies, mini-cans of fruits and puddings—suggest that people don't eat "three square meals" any longer, but are living on more or less continuous snacking. It follows from this that consumers should have some way to evaluate the nutrition in specific products and that the industry has some responsibility to ensure that the foods people buy contribute to good health. It would certainly be wise to require nutrition labeling and nutrition advertising that go beyond vapid recommendations that people eat a balanced diet from among the four basic food groups. But it does not follow that unnutritious foods should be banned or, as Choate suggests, that the number of food commercials on television be limited arbitrarily to four an hour. The justification for that provision in Choate's code seemed to be that television is dangerously influential and that it has replaced mother as "Junior's principal nutrition educator" (his phrase). That may be true, but if a food product is legally sold and no one has made a case for removing it from the market as a health hazard there is no reasonable basis for limiting the frequency or timing of commercials.

Similarly, there is no self-evident reason to insist that every advertised "prize" make a "positive contribution to the child's improved physical health." Apart from the obvious problem of defining "positive contribution" and "physical health," the rule is whimsical and authoritarian. Must every toy be productive of muscle to be worth a child's time? A sugar-tooth decay rule is probably superfluous. Surely parents and children who see all those toothpaste commercials know by now that sugar contributes to tooth decay? Is it essential that every Hershey bar commercial contain a warning, "This candy may be hazardous to your teeth"? To require such nonsense is to assume that parents are not only miserably informed but incapable of out-arguing the television set.

At the base of Choate's code is a desire to reduce the power of television commercials. It would be naive to think advertisers or broadcasters would share this desire. And it would be frightening were the government to force the code's restrictions. Food advertising is not pornography; children do not need to be saved from it so long as it does not make patently false claims. And when advertising is deceptive, we all need to be protected from it.

The same is true of mayhem on the tube. The best that can be said of all the studies of television violence and its effect on children is that they are inconclusive. Frank Stanton, then president of the Columbia Broadcasting System (CBS), told the Eisenhower Commission on the Causes and Prevention of Violence that "no one in the thirty-odd years I have been in the business has come up with a technique or methodology that would let you get a fix on this impact [of violence]." It's not to be assumed that the television networks have ever seriously wanted conclusive evidence, especially of a negative sort, since a final answer, if one were possible, might have a dramatic and unwanted effect on network programming.

Robert K. Baker, an antitrust lawyer who served as co-director of the Eisenhower Commission's task force on media and violence, did an extensive review of network programming standards and practices and concluded that standards are "weak because they appear to be based on little more than a fear of losing viewers." Baker's tabulation, however, reflected badly on the industry, which has for more than fifteen years hidden behind the inconclusiveness of the data, while never actively sponsoring research that might yield positive answers. Instead, it has played a game of promise and delay.

In 1954 Harold E. Fellows told a Senate subcommittee that the National Association of Broadcasters, of which he was then president, would undertake a survey of the impact of programming on children. In 1961 James T. Aubrey, who was later fired as president of CBS, told the Senate that the NAB had asked CBS to do the study, which would indeed cover the effects of violence. The nine-year effort, published finally in 1963, turned out to be nothing more than a survey of parents' beliefs about what television violence did to their children. It offered, in the words of its author, "no direct evidence." The networks' next stab at a study—this one done by a group called the Joint Committee for Research on Television and Children—produced in the late sixties an analysis of the inadequacies of the research on this matter. CBS used the results to reiterate that the evidence is inconclusive.

A good deal of thought has been given to the subject of violence, but not by the networks. The American Broadcasting Company (ABC) and the National Broadcasting Company (NBC), which participated with the United States Department of Health, Education, and Welfare (HEW) in the Joint Committee, had, according to the Eisenhower Commission report, "sponsored no original research." Robert Baker said "ABC executives feel that it is pointless for them to sponsor research because any findings which this work might produce would be suspect." ABC itself said "research should be done from an objective standpoint and one that the public would be satisfied with as being done objectively, rather than that which is directly financed by our particular company."

It may not even be possible, as former CBS president Frank Stanton argues, to devise methods for finding correct answers, but the networks' and the broadcasters' association's sporadic attempts to control violence in programming have been designed to keep it to an inexact "minimum."

The Senate Commerce Communications Subcommittee, under the leadership of Senator John Pastore, has taken up the cudgels in support of research that would find "meaningful answers." The Eisenhower Violence Commission was of the opinion that children do learn aggressive behavior from television, that habitually viewing violence on television "increases likelihood" of aggressive behavior, and that to the extent that television violence is depicted as "wrong" it is less likely to adversely affect children's behavior. Beyond that, the Commission's staff study recommended—you guessed it—additional research. That is where the matter rests.

Before the Commission study was published, an impatient Senator Pastore wrote to then HEW Secretary Robert Finch asking for a study that would once and for all offer useful data on the harm done by a medium which, by one estimate, the average eighteen-year-old has watched for more than twenty-two thousand hours. He wanted the National Institute of Mental Health at HEW to do the job, as it had on smoking and lung cancer. Pastore's suggestion got a quick favorable response from HEW; the department would sponsor a million dollars' worth of fresh research. Then it was disclosed that the three networks would be allowed to pass on the membership of the study committee. Forty allegedly qualified candidates were submitted to the networks. Seven were blackballed; the networks considered them unqualified on the grounds that some of them had already studied television violence and come to conclusions hostile to the networks. Albert Bandura, one of the seven and a professor at Stanford, had published research suggesting that children become more aggressive after watching violence on television. So had Leonard Berkowitz, a psychology professor from the University of Wisconsin.

The blackballing would not have come to light had it not been for Dougles A. Fuchs, a hundred-dollar-a-day consultant to the HEW committee with the title of Research Coordinator. He also revealed that several members of the committee finally selected were or had been in the employ of the networks. The revelation displeased Dr. Eli Rubenstein, who as deputy director of the National Institute of Mental Health headed the research group. For the four weeks prior to Fuchs' resignation Rubenstein refused to speak to him and treated him, in Fuchs' words, as a "nonperson."

Senator Pastore, of course, got wind of the charges and wrote HEW to ask about the fishy appointment procedure. He got in reply an oddly worded defense. HEW contended that the networks had been allowed to veto candidates because if they were satisfied with the composition of the committee they couldn't carp later if they didn't like the final report. The letter did not explain how the government would be able to justify the report if it let the industry off the hook. It was hardly surprising that the million-dollar committee concluded early in 1972 that TV programming does not have a bad effect on most children. Violence on television *might* influence *certain* children who were otherwise predisposed to aggressive behavior.

HEW said the same procedure was used with the cigarette study; the tobacco companies were allowed a veto. It is true that the tobacco companies had been consulted, but so had the American Cancer Society. Perhaps that is why no tobacco industry people served on the cancer committee. No organized group stands opposed to the television industry; thus no one on the other side was given similar veto powers. The result was a biased panel. ABC's stated belief that the public wouldn't believe the results of research sponsored by the industry, with its inevitable vested interest in the outcome, seems peculiarly relevant to the HEW study.

Great adventure will do as well as shoot-'em-dead melodrama to con the consumer in buying something he may or may not want or like. The national television networks thought the routine moon landing of Apollo 14 newsworthy enough to begin their live color coverage of the event at 3:00 A.M. on a Friday, an hour no one but a space nut would consider devoting to television. Commercial advertisers went along. Gulf Oil, a major space contractor, sponsored every second of NBC's coverage of Apollo 14. Was the attention and the sponsorship worth the expense? I don't know if viewers at large were as bored by the lengthy coverage as my play group was, or whether they question as I do the repetition of costly moon landings while other scientific and social programs go begging. But whether viewers are bored or not, the networks are committed to space. It's always possible that a moon shot will fail, and that contingency adds drama to an event whose smooth success otherwise stimulates ennui. The advertising executives of General Foods obviously think that the $20 billion the public has spent on manned space flight is good for their imitation orange juice, Tang, which is drunk by the astronauts. (The astronauts have said more than once that they don't much care for the food up there.)

A number of products sell themselves through association with the space program—Tang and Space Food Sticks (Pillsbury), for example. The Goodyear Tire & Rubber Company ran full-page ads in the *Wall Street Journal* under the title, "Some down-to-earth facts about the first tires on the moon." The tire people are persuaded that consumers are impressed by a product used in space, because NASA wouldn't use materials as unreliable as the stuff earthmen have to buy. But if the space program has proved nothing else, it is that no amount of advertised value-by-association assures equipment completely free of defects in workmanship and operation.

The chief earthly by-product of space (other than Corningware and Teflon) is entertainment of a sort, and advertisers see to it that while we are being entertained we are sold. Heroism in space sells goods (whoever made the golf ball that went to the moon with Alan Shepard could not lose on the deal). Retired space people—themselves for sale—make good pitchmen for products and services (e.g., Walter Shirra speaking for the American railroads, Colonel John "Shorty" Powers for Oldsmobile). Some time ago I spent a day at NASA looking at the file they keep of products exploiting the space program. The typical astronaut, it would seem, wears an Accutron or an Omega ("the watch that orbited in outer space"), brushes his teeth with a Py-co-pay ("the toothbrush selected by NASA"), and of course drinks Tang ("aboard every space flight since Gemini IV"). He takes pictures with a Hasselblad on Kodak film.

Where astronauts have not used a product itself, there is still an opportunity for a tie-in. A shoe company had a "walk weightless" campaign. A department store pictured a little boy praying for the astronauts' safe return. A car manufacturer captioned a photo of a fellow in a roomy car, "man in space." A cereal producer put pictures of United States space exploits on its boxes of breakfast food. A pharmaceutical company illustrated advertising for a diuretic drug with NASA photos of a space walk. The drug had nothing to do with the space program; it was seized by the Food and Drug Administration for deceptive advertising.)

NASA refuses to allow astronauts to endorse products; NASA contractors are asked to submit advertising for a check of technical accuracy; and NASA photographs are released with the caption, "for noncommercial, noncopyrightable public information use. Written permission must be received from NASA if used in advertising." But such procedures are often ignored by advertisers. If an ad agency submits a proposed layout to NASA, the space agency may say yes and it may say no, but if the agency chooses not to follow that procedure there is little NASA can do about it. "We could go to court," says Walter Pennino, a NASA public relations official, "but you ask yourself if it's worth it." NASA settles for sending polite letters to advertisers who use its photographs, which are freely available to the public but not for unauthorized commercial use.

More often than not, a company told by NASA not to use a NASA tie-in will comply, as did the manufacturer of a chintzy souvenir liquor bottle emblazoned with the faces of three of the astronauts. He was told that the astronauts have a legal proprietary right to their names, faces, and voices, and that facsimiles of their faces cannot be used without permission, and NASA wasn't giving him permission.

NASA, in fact, is rather happy for a plug. Space-oriented advertising gives a boost to the space program and helps get further appropriations out of Congress. The only time NASA gets perturbed is when a company that makes a small part employed in the program uses a photo in its advertising that implies that the company is responsible for the whole space-craft. "Prime contractors take a damn dim view of that," says Pennino. On the whole, however, "advertisers keep each other honest."

NASA's files, which include an estimated five hundred new applications for permissions each year, are full of evidence of tie-in advertising which strains the truth. The Py-co-pay toothbrush, for instance, was bought by NASA, but when the ad using the line "the toothbrush selected by NASA" was published, Py-co-pay had never actually been used in space. The astronauts chewed a dentifrice gum (Dentyne?). "Just because some procurement officer goes out and buys shelf items at a drugstore doesn't mean they were *selected*," says Walter Pennino.

In yet another case NASA got an angry letter from the vice-president of the Longines-Wittnauer watch company complaining that his firm's watches hadn't been invited to compete with Omega for use in space. He wondered if NASA had a policy of permitting companies to make "trumped up and puffed up claims that ride on the reputation" of the space agency. NASA replied that it had examined the watches of four companies, including Longines-Wittnauer. During temperature, humidity, and pressure tests, the crystal on the Longines-Wittnauer popped out, so NASA ended up using Omega. The watch *had* been considered and rejected. The company was mad anyway; its competitor got the tie-in.

The question the watch company official asked is valid. NASA quite justifiably cannot dictate to advertisers. "We're not," as Pennino says, "a regulatory agency."

But consumers can read and presumably discern for themselves whether a product exploiting the space program is any more worth buying for the association, tenuous as it often is. I suspect in most cases the right answer is that it is not.

Whether something is worth buying or not is a question that has undergone a qualified change in recent years, in part because of the rise of the credit card. The best things in life are *not* free, but they may seem to be. Indeed, today there is no longer any need to buy credit-card insurance to protect against the unauthorized use of lost or stolen credit cards. It isn't necessary because Congress in 1970 passed a law that limits the cardholder's liability in a loss case to fifty dollars. Whether or not you notify the issuer of a card that it's been lost, fifty dollars is the most you'll ever have to pay per card, even if someone fraudulently runs up thousands of dollars in bills in your name.

American Express, the largest of the so-called Travel and Entertainment (T&E) card companies, had a very odd way of informing its customers of their rights under this law. With one month's billing statements, American Express sent its members a small pamphlet explaining that "if your American Express Money Card is lost or stolen, as an American Express Card member you have an automatic $50 deductible liability protection FREE!"

The American Express description suggested that the service was a favor the company was doing for the more than 3.5 million people who pay fifteen dollars apiece each year to carry an American Express card.

That's hardly the case. It isn't largesse; it's the law. James Thompson, an American Express official in New York, explained that even before the law was passed American Express insured members against losses of more than one hundred dollars (now the legal limit is fifty dollars). "We weren't required to do this; it was our policy. We were the first in the industry to come out with this service." But isn't it deceptive now to portray a service required by federal law as something offered out of the kindness of American Express' corporate heart? "Geez, I don't know," replied Mr. Thompson. "I suppose there's a million ways you could express it."

American Express ran television spot commercials in major markets throughout the country, advertising credit cards. In one of the commercials an actor named Paul Richards read the following script:

> You know there are hundreds of different credit cards—department stores, bank cards, oil companies. You may have a dozen in your own wallet. All are different from this—the American Express Money Card. For example, the Money Card has no automatic finance charges. Most other cards charge up to one-and-a-half percent per month on your unpaid balance—an annual rate of 18 percent. Now maybe you don't blink at finance charges. But if you do, remember, the Money Card has no such automatic finance charges. You pay an annual $15 fee—period.

That's straightforward, or is it?

The commercial intrigued me, and apparently it interested a lot of other people as well, because according to James Thompson, American Express got letters from customers who had used their American Express cards to buy airplane tickets and had paid finance charges amounting to 12 percent. What is this about "no automatic finance charges," anyway? Mr. Thompson explained that, strictly speaking, the commercial is accurate. There are no "automatic" charges. But airline tickets and tours are a slight exception to the normal workings of American Express. If a traveler wants to spread out payments for charges made with his card, he specifically arranges for a time-payment plan, including finance charges, when he purchases his tickets. Otherwise, unless arrangements are made for deferred payments, American Express clients are required to pay off the total balance printed on each monthly statement on receipt of the bill. "That is stipulated in the contract you get when you get the card."

So that is another difference between American Express and the hundreds of other credit cards mentioned in the television commercial. Bank cards, department store cards, and some other cards, which you don't have to pay an annual fee to get, make their profits from extended payments. The customary 18 percent finance charge is the source of their profit. American Express and the two other major Travel and Entertainment Cards—Carte Blanche and Diners Club—charge an annual fee. They make their profit from this fee and also from charging business establishments that honor the cards a percentage on the amount of each credit card purchase ranging from 2 to 6 percent. (This, incidentally, is the hidden cost of credit which all consumers pay whether or not they use credit cards. Next time you pay cash for a meal in a restaurant that honors credit cards, ask if they will give you a discount for paying cash.)

American Express chooses not to get involved in re-volving credit, so it charges no "automatic finance charges." (The typical card holder, James Thompson says, is a businessman on an expense account. His firm pays the bill and can afford, indeed prefers, to pay the total outstanding balance each month, so the mat-ter of late payments and partial payments tends not to arise.) But nobody who extends credit assesses finance charges when a customer pays off immediately after receiving the bill. Certainly bank cards, depart-ment stores, and oil companies don't. Is the advantage of American Express over these other cards to be found then in a permissive attitude toward people who skip payments or make partial payments? Is that what Paul Richards means when he says on television that other cards "charge up to one-and-a-half percent per month on your unpaid balance" but American Express doesn't? No, he doesn't mean that at all, which be-comes clear when you ask American Express what happens to customers who don't keep their accounts current. "They get dunned," admits James Thompson. They get a succession of dunning letters, which begin politely and become increasingly more threatening until finally after about ninety days American Express cancels the credit card. Efforts at collection continue.

The contract you sign when you get an American Ex-press card states: "Member promises to pay the amount of any and all purchases charged to the ac-count immediately upon receipt of Amexco's monthly statement. . . . A deliquency charge of 1½ percent per month [18 percent annually] may be added on any amount 60 days in arrears if not received prior to the next monthly billing date. Court costs plus attorney fees of 15 percent of the then unpaid balance may be added to the Member's account if referred to an attorney for collection." In other words, if you don't pay up in sixty days, American Express threatens to charge you an 18 percent late fee, before they send their lawyer after you.

So, if you can't make late payments or partial payments without getting into what looks like trouble, what is Paul Richards talking about in that straightforward-sounding TV commercial? Tim Sickinger, the account supervisor who handled American Express ads for Ogilvy & Mather, the New York advertising agency, would offer no rebuttal to the suggestion that the commercial was deceptive and exploited a distinction without a difference between American Express and other credit cards. "We obviously believe there is a difference," he said, "or we wouldn't have written the commercial this way."

When a theater critic thinks a play is bad, he says so, without regard to the economic interests he may be harming. If the play folds after one performance, that's tough. Producers lose money and actors lose jobs, but their fate is considered less important than the right of the reviewer to comment freely and fairly and the right of the public to read honest criticism.

The tradition of open expression in criticizing the arts does not, unfortunately, carry over into other areas. Product reviews—the sort of thing *Consumer Reports* does so well in rating goods on a brand-by-brand basis—are not well received. In fact, critical mention of brand names on the air and in print is relatively new. Before Ralph Nader slew the Corvair, newspapers and especially broadcasters often covered consumer stories as if brand names were dirty words. Part of the reluctance was a fear of lost advertising, part was a fear of lawsuits, and part was motivated by a sense of decency. (One should have evidence that a product is shoddy before one says anything that will hurt the business.)

Fortunately, the media have become a good deal less skittish about "naming names." Ralph Ginzburg, to cite one example, wrote a letter to the editor of *Time* to congratulate the magazine on its journalistic integrity. What so pleased Ginzburg was that *Time* had published a nasty review of Ginzburg's new newsletter, *Moneysworth,* in the same issue in which Ginzburg had bought a full-page ad for *Moneysworth.* Such journalistic courage, if that's what it is, was rare in the days newspapers regularly promised potential advertisers a certain amount of favorable, manufactured "news" coverage (grand openings, sales) for placing advertising with the paper.

Still, now and then you run into old brick walls. Joe Franklin, a radio personality on radio station WOR in New York, is an old-movie buff and the sort of interviewer who, during commercials, asks his guests what he should ask them next. I spent forty minutes with Mr. Franklin once, talking about consumer abuses. Before the show I was told I could say anything I pleased, but that I couldn't mention the names of companies or product brands. It was a mental exercise I wouldn't care to repeat. At one point I let slip the words "General Motors" and felt exceedingly guilty.

Television, more than radio, has a hangup about mentioning brand names, though there are exceptions. Marshall Efron's demonstration (on "The Great American Dream Machine," a National Educational Television series that premiered in 1970) of how to make a Morton lemon cream pie using nothing but a chemistry set (no lemons, no eggs, no cream) was a devastating exception.

Frank Pollock, the Executive Assistant to the Director of Consumers Union (CU), recounted to me some experiences Consumers Union has had in trying to alert the public (via television) to dangerous toys. Once the late Morris Kaplan, a CU official, had been invited to appear on a WABC-TV (New York) program called the "A.M. Show." He'd been told in advance that he could identify the dangerous toys by name, but when he got to the studio he saw that the toys he planned to display had masking tape obscuring their names. The production crew cited "legal problems" and would not dispense with the tape until Kaplan threatened to walk out on the show just as it was about to begin. He was thus able to identify the toys, but only by making a fuss.

WABC-TV ran an item on a news program about Consumers Union's attempts to get stronger enforcement of the Toy Safety Act and ran an interview with a CU representative, but omitted mention of the specific toys CU had found to be hazardous. The Today Show, broadcast nationally on NBC, invited Mr. Kaplan to discuss toy safety, but cancelled out when informed that he intended to single out brands. Subsequently, the show's producers said the appearance had been cancelled because the subject had been so well covered elsewhere. Oddly enough, Consumers Union had no such problems on other shows. The NBC Nightly News, WNBC news, NBC's Monitor, WCBS news, and WABC-FM all ran stories in which toys were identified by name.

The names of cigarettes are, of course, banned on television, and, when cigarette commercials were forced off television and radio in January 1971, many people—including some in the tobacco industry—wondered where all the available advertising money would go. Since cigarette companies planned to stay in the business, they would have to look for ingenious new selling devices. Whatever means they chose, it was clear that the industry would be denounced by the anticancer interests—the people who believe that if cigarettes kill people and therefore it is not considered to be in the public interest to advertise them on television, then it's not in the public interest to advertise them at all.

There was immediate speculation (denied) that the tobacco companies would put out pipe tobaccos with the same brand names as their cigarettes and advertise *them* on TV. The industry began to take an interest in underwriting sporting events held in unlikely places like Winston-Salem. Virginia Slims sponsored a press luncheon in New York devoted to the subject of women's liberation. The American Tobacco Company sent out in the mail free samples of Silva Thins. Cigarette advertising doubled in *Time, Life,* and *Newsweek.* None of these new routes to promote cigarettes and smoking escaped notice or criticism, and there is a growing feeling among critics that cigarette advertising in all forms should be banned. Until that happens, if it does, the tobacco industry is having a field day experimenting with new advertising modes and media.

The Castagna Electronics Corporation in Brooklyn, New York, tried to interest the cigarette people in a device that would let them, in a sense, continue broadcasting commercials despite the ban on television and radio advertising. The invention, the technical name of which is the Audio Commercial Message Repeating Unit (ACMRU), would not make use of the public's airwaves, however, and therefore not violate the law. It is a talking vending machine, or rather an instrument that allows vending machines to say what's on their minds. It sits unobtrusively atop an ordinary vendor and looks like an illuminated advertising sign. But behind the façade is a cassette tape player primed to deliver a twenty-second jingle whenever anyone drops a coin into the machine.

According to its developer, the device can be programmed with old, otherwise unusable, radio commercials or with something tailor-made for the ACMRU. The message can be repeated, or a slightly different message can be delivered each time the machine is activated, until the two-hour tape is completed and begins to repeat. A. Frederick Greenberg, the president of Castagna, thinks it would be better to use a variety of messages, so that customers won't get bored and people who have to work near the machines won't go out of their minds. One charm of the device, Greenberg says, is that the tapes can be recorded to do all sorts of things including delivering occasional little pitches for the business where the vending machine is located; for example, "This is Joe, the bartender. Now that you've got your cigarettes, come back to the bar." Conceivably the machines could be programmed so as not to release the merchandise until the message has been played or not to allow the selection of a cigarette brand until the ACMRU has gotten in its two-cents' worth. One thing that can't be done with the machine is to turn it off.

Greenberg claimed in a release to the New York financial community that there are "millions" of vending machines in the United States, 250,000 of which are in "prime high-traffic areas," where many people pass by and where the machines aren't likely to be vandalized. This is his target market, and "major cigarette manufacturers" have "enthusiastically greeted" the ACMRU and are "considering purchasing" the machines to test-market the idea. The manufacturers, under Greenberg's scheme, would own the tape machine and pay the vending machine company a fee for marrying the two devices. With thirty-two "basic slots" or pigeon-holes dispensing cigarette packs in an average machine, the company with the ACMRU would have a presumed competitive advantage over others.

Greenberg stands to make money from his machine, so perhaps it is too much to expect him to have any compunctions about "noise pollution," the "invasion of privacy," or "public health." He's in the sound business. What is surprising is that the cigarette companies might want to chance alienating people who aren't accustomed to having vending machines talk back to them and who are smokers in any event. (Who would want to sell his cigarettes in a machine that delivers a pitch only for a competitor's product?) The whole thing is preposterous. But Greenberg says that three companies—specifically, American Tobacco, Lorillard, and Liggett & Myers—have seen his machine, like it, and plan to buy a number of the units to test. We shall see.

I have on my desk a small white carton containing two packages of Silva Thins, which came in the mail as an unsolicited gift from The American Tobacco Company. Since I quit smoking but still have the urge, I am tempted to smoke them, but instead I'll probably do as the engraved note that came with the sample suggests and "pass this gift along to a friend" who smokes, or (my own idea) throw them away. I don't quite know what to think about The American Tobacco Company's largesse, since, as the printed warning on the box and on the enclosed packs states, "The Surgeon General has determined that cigarette smoking is dangerous to your health." The mailing of certain firearms is restricted by law. But slow death of the sort cigarettes cause is another matter. Representative William D. Ford of Michigan introduced a bill in the House of Representatives that would prohibit the mailing of unsolicited cigarettes, but barring its eventual passage the Silva Thins promotion appears to be legal. (The tobacco companies used to give out sample cigarettes to soldiers and college students, but several years ago they adopted an informal code banning the practice. Now, with no way to advertise on television or radio, "sampling" has been revived.)

Congressman Ford, a number of state agencies, the American Cancer Society, and the Clearinghouse on Smoking and Health have received complaints from sample recipients in Florida, California, Michigan, Maryland, Virginia, Rhode Island, and Washington. A

Cancer Society spokesman says he heard "from all over the country." The protest focused primarily on the likelihood that the free samples would fall into the hands of children.

In every state but Louisiana it is illegal to sell cigarettes to minors, defined variously as persons under sixteen, seventeen, eighteen, and twenty-one. If such laws were enforced, one could argue that the promiscuous mailing of unsolicted cigarettes violates those laws, since it's not possible to weed out children from recipients. It was reported that in its Florida mailing The American Tobacco Company hoped to resolve that problem by addressing samples to "adult residents."

Since cigarettes are seldom kept under lock and key, since laws against sale to minors are commonly winked at, and since vending machines have no scruples, it is ridiculous to think—whether or not samples are sent through the mails—that it could ever be possible to keep children and cigarettes away from each other. Drug laws don't prevent traffic in marijuana, the sale and use of which are punishable by imprisonment. So it's a vain hope that cigarettes can be any more closely regulated by laws that are less stringent.

It obviously makes sense as a matter of public policy to discourage smoking as much as possible. Hence the prohibition of television and radio advertising. (Sending out samples is a far greater threat to public health than television advertising, and it's directed at the same source—the home.) But public policy vis-à-vis cigarettes is remarkably ambivalent. While the Surgeon General warns people not to smoke and Congress requires that cigarettes not be advertised on the air, the Agriculture Department subsidizes tobacco growers and actively promotes the export of American tobacco products. Cigarettes are legally sold and legally advertised in the print media, and, so long as they remain available, there is very little chance that a substantial number of persons will either stop or fail to start smoking.

The United States presumably could ban all advertising of cigarettes, cigars, and smoking tobacco (as is done in Singapore), although regulating printed advertising runs up against First Amendment problems. Congress could revive Prohibition—this time for cigarettes —and institute an outright ban on their sale and use. But that Noble Experiment does not suggest its repetition.

Although the tobacco companies are diversifying their businesses and changing their corporate names (American Tobacco is now "a division of American Brands, Inc.") against the awful prospect of dwindling sales, few responsible critics expect the companies to be put out of business by fiat. For one thing, there are 41 million cigarette addicts. Although some of them might welcome the bolstering effect banning cigarettes would have on their willpower, many others, including six hundred thousand farm families growing tobacco, would scream bloody murder were the government to make their habits and their livelihood a criminal enterprise.

It is illegal, thanks to something called the Delaney Clause of the Food and Drug Law, to sell any food product or medication containing cancer-causing agents. The Delaney Clause is acceptable because it does not have a massive effect on economic interests and on consumer demand for products. In the abstract, no one would wish to consume or allow to be sold anything known to cause cancer. But somehow with cigarettes things are different.

There is a whole class of "crimes without victims" (including gambling, prostitution, sexual aberrations, and drug use), the practice of which primarily harms only the "criminal." To make such vices illegal (cigarette smoking included) does little to eradicate the behavior. It just makes life more difficult for the person with the vice who must cope not only with his impulses but with the possibility that he will be jailed for giving in to temptation.

But whereas criminal penalties seem ineffective and barbaric, it is another matter for government to encourage vice officially, and that includes subsidies to tobacco growers, incentives to foreign buyers, permitting the use of public airwaves to sell dangerous goods, and the use of the mails to distribute samples of cigarettes. The Silva Thins I have on my desk were sent by third-class mail, at a cost of less than four cents to The American Tobacco Company, a rate subsidized by taxpayers. It is not out of order to insist, at the very least, that the cigarette people pay first-class rates (which they probably couldn't afford to do). Congressman Ford thinks it legitimate to prohibit cigarette mailings, if, as is the case, the government thinks it right to ban pornographic mailings and the shipment of fireworks. Making things tough for the cigarette industry is, under the circumstances, in the public interest. But it won't prevent a child, or anyone who wants to take up smoking, from having his way.

# 6
# drugs on the market

Hayfever sufferers take a drug called Chlor-Trimeton to alleviate symptoms of runny nose and itchy eyes. Unless his illness is limited to certain seasons of the year a sufferer is likely to take a twelve-milligram tablet (made by the Schering Corporation) twice a day, every day, year in and year out. Chlor-Trimeton is an excellent and effective drug, and it has the advantage over other antihistamines of not making you as drowsy. You can get it only with a prescription. Chlor-Trimeton is one of the fifty most frequently prescribed medicines; elderly patients alone spend more than $2 million a year for it.

A thousand timed-release tablets of Chlor-Trimeton would take a chronic hayfever sufferer who takes it morning and night exactly one year, four months, and two weeks to go through. Druggists buy Chlor-Trimeton wholesale for $50.28 per thousand tablets. A prescription might be for thirty tablets. How does that work out for the patient? A typical pharmacist marks up the drug by 67 percent of his wholesale cost, in order to make a profit of 40 percent on the retail price.

He may add as much as one dollar for every prescription he fills. This means that he may sell thirty Chlor-Trimeton tablets for $3.50. I noted that two drugstores that advertise discount prices in Washington, D.C., were selling thirty tablets for $2.55 and $2.83 respectively. At the lowest of these rates patients who buy thirty tablets at a time would eventually spend $84.00 for a thousand. The same store would fill a single prescription for one thousand tablets for $60.00.

It isn't necessary to go about your drug shopping in this way. You can buy the drug in quantity from a drug supplier by the drug's *generic* name. The scientific or generic name for Chlor-Trimeton is chlorpheniramine maleate. It takes a while to get down the pronunciation, but familiarizing yourself with the name saves money. Chlorpheniramine is the same drug that Schering packages as Chlor-Trimeton. But when a physician writes a prescription for Chlor-Trimeton, the druggist must (in forty-four states) fill it with Schering's product. He does so because of antisubstitution laws enacted in most states as the result of lobbying pressure from the Pharmaceutical Manufacturers Association, the trade group that represents the brand-name manufacturers. If, however, the doctor writes chlorpheniramine, a pharmacist is free to fill the prescription with the same drug made by any of a number of different drug companies, many of which sell it cheaply.

Any licensed drug company can make chlorpheniramine; no one any longer has exclusive rights to its manufacture. (Seventeen years is the longest a company can maintain its monopoly on a drug.) Schering has a competitive advantage over its cheaper competitors, however, because doctors, druggists, and patients are familiar with its tradenames. Since the names are expensively and heavily advertised and the company's salesmen give samples to doctors, many physicians write in the brand name on prescriptions from habit.

Also, the Pharmaceutical Manufacturers Association has claimed that generics aren't as safe as (or aren't therapeutically equivalent to) brand-name drugs. Don't believe it. In 1968 the Department of Health, Education, and Welfare assigned the above claim for investigation by a task force on prescription drugs. After fourteen months of study, assisted by two hundred expert consultants, HEW found that "except in rare instances, drugs which are chemically equivalent and which meet all official standards, can be expected to produce essentially the same biological or clinical effects."

So there's no good reason for the doctor not to write chlorpheniramine on the prescription blank. You can then take the prescription on a comparison shopping trip, leaving it with the druggist who will give you the best price on generic chlorpheniramine. If your hayfever is chronic and you need to take something regularly for some time, you can ask the doctor to specify a large quantity. Then you can send the prescription to a pharmaceutical supply company, which will sell it to you, in effect, at wholesale prices. (The ABC Drug Company, 171-08 39th Avenue, Flushing, New York 11358, will fill a prescription for one thousand, twelve-milligram tablets of chlorpheniramine maleate for $7.75, including fifty cents for postage and handling. That's about 13 percent of the $60 a "discount" drugstore will charge you for Chlor-Trimeton.)

What is true for chlorpheniramine is true for scores of other drugs available in both brand-name and generic form. The ABC Drug Company is just one of many suppliers. The best source of information on buying generics is *The New Handbook of Prescription Drugs* by Dr. Richard Burack of the Harvard Medical School.

The Pharmaceutical Manufacturers Association (PMA), which represents the prominent makers of prescription drugs, is one of the most visible and successful lobby organizations in Washington. It doesn't admit to lobbying in its publicity material, but it has lobbyists registered with Congress. Anyone who doesn't believe they do their jobs well should consult Senator Gaylord Nelson, whose hearings on generic drugs have shown that many of PMA's industry apologies are only partial truth.

The Pharmaceutical Manufacturers are ably represented in the nation's capital by C. Joseph Stetler, whose labors on behalf of the drug companies include a regular poop session for journalists. In a letter to press people, Stetler said: "Better communications is the goal of every organization—and PMA is no exception. So we are going to try something that we hope will be useful to you and helpful to us. Every three months or so we will schedule an informal coffee and doughnuts session where you will be invited to drop by and ask questions of myself and our staff. We aren't promising any hot news; we simply want to be available to provide information."

It is very nice of Mr. Stetler to offer to help set the press straight about the drug business; PMA has a good deal of setting straight to do. In his *New Handbook of Prescription Drugs,* Richard Burack describes in some detail how the drug industry has fought the new interest in generic drugs, generally taking the position that brand-name drugs are likely to be safer than the same drugs marketed by a variety of companies under chemical or scientific names.

PMA has disseminated its view widely, once in a multipage ad masquerading as an article in the *Readers Digest.* PMA on one occasion paid five economics professors forty thousand dollars to testify before a congressional committee. The intent of all this is to convince Congress, physicians, patients, and the press that generics are risky and that faith should be placed in the reputations of the major drug firms. PMA has even been known to allege that drug prices are going down!

Dr. Burack deftly demolishes all of these claims. On the safety issue he cites the HEW 1968 drug study, showing that in all but rare cases "drugs which are chemically equivalent and which meet all official standards" have the same therapeutic effects: "There is at present no known reason to suspect any given generic drug of being less effective than its expensive brand-name counterpart."

PMA once published an ad asserting that there is "no generic equivalent" for reputation. A prescription for a brand name "expresses confidence in the manufacturer's integrity, uncompromising production standards, quality control, and his dedication to the public welfare." The clear inference is that generics are less trustworthy, less safe. Why then do recalls by the Food and Drug Administration (FDA) occur more often with the famous brand-name drugs? In 1967, for instance, *all* major recalls of adulterated, mislabeled, substandard, and "violative" drugs involved brand-name products. The same year more than 32 percent of PMA manufacturers sold drugs that violated FDA standards, as opposed to 15.5 percent of non-PMA manufacturers.

Are brand-name drugs more expensive because of lavish research by responsible PMA companies? No. What is lavish is their advertising. They spend twenty-five cents of every sales dollar on advertising (ten cents on research). Their ad expenditures average out to three thousand dollars per doctor per year. Despite their costs of doing business, the drug companies are the highest profit industry in the United States. Profits based on sales are consistently more than twice that of all the rest of the five hundred most profitable United States companies. Profits based on invested capital run at least 50 percent higher.

Finally there is the matter of drug prices. Are they going down? On the contrary, the average prescription written in 1967 cost $3.43, about 50 percent more than the average prescription fourteen years before.

The Pharmaceutical Manufacturers Association, servant and protector of expensive brand-name drugs, is especially sensitive to public statements it fears might loosen the grip it has on doctors and patients. Skilled in publicity, PMA and its president, C. Joseph Stetler, answer criticisms with counterclaims that more often than not obscure the issue and discredit the critic.

Richard Burack's *Handbook of Prescription Drugs* particularly annoyed Mr. Stetler, because it told the public how to economize on drugs by buying them generically from manufacturers, most of whom aren't members of PMA. Burack's book had an immense impact in Washington. Gaylord Nelson was spurred to undertake his exhaustive investigations of drug prices. The book and Nelson's hearings led to the establishment of a government task force on prescription drugs. Its report in 1968 corroborated Burack's claims for generics and showed that "prescribing practices are apparently even more chaotic and industry control of the [medical] profession more extensive than I had earlier realized." The task force conclusion that "chemically equivalent drugs . . . produce essentially the same results" has eased a lot of minds and saved money for patients who, with their doctors' blessings, no longer rely on expensive drugs simply because the manufacturer's name is familiar.

One would not expect the Pharmaceutical Manufacturers Association to send Dr. Burack a thank-you note for his contribution, since the public interest is not PMA's. But when Burack's book was reissued in an expanded edition (twice the length, with an enlarged drug list, updated prices, listings by both generic and brand name, a section on prescribing for children, and a list of the two hundred most prescribed drugs), Mr. Stetler reacted with exceptional peevishness: "Drug prices have changed far less, relatively, than Dr. Burack's book from first edition (1967) at $4.95 to second edition (1970) at $7.95. The consumer pays 60 percent more now for a 'molecular modification' of a book published three years ago!"

As an investment counselor and also as a corrective to PMA, Burack's book seems to me a good buy. It saves us from leaning exclusively on PMA's official version of the truth about drugs. To prove that some such corrective is needed, here are some samples from PMA and Mr. Stetler, with annotations:

"The PMA does *not* claim that 'brand name drugs' are more likely to be safe than those sold under their generic or common names." (That's news. Ben Gordon, the chief economist of Senator Nelson's subcommittee, informed me that Stetler and PMA have continually made safety claims for brand-name drugs and implied dangers in generics. A PMA magazine ad I have filed away urges doctors to prescribe brand-name drugs. It claims "there is no generic equivalent for reputation; it cannot be bought or duplicated.")

"The Pharmaceutical Manufacturers Association is not a lobbying organization." (This statement appeared in the PMA Drug Industry Fact Book. What Mr. Stetler means is that although PMA has two lobbyists registered with Congress it has many other activities as well.)

"The increase in the average prescription expenditure must be modest by any standard." (The Consumer Price Index, on which Mr. Stetler bases this claim, monitors only fourteen drugs and fails to include the newest and costliest ones. Between 1953 and 1967, according to Burack's figures, the price of an average prescription increased 50 percent.)

"The current ratio of research and development expenditures to pharmaceutical sales by PMA member firms is 11.4 percent—by far the highest of any industry. PMA firms also lead all industries in percentage used for basic research." (Here Mr. Stetler is trying to counteract Burack's claim that one reason drugs are so expensive is that drug companies spend so much of their sales income on advertising. Mr. Stetler says it's "nowhere near as much" as 25 percent, but he doesn't say how much it is. His stress on research is interesting. Henry Gadsden, the president of Merck, one of the large pharmaceutical manufacturers, has predicted that in a given ten-year period the large drug companies will produce no more than three or four major new products. Will that, perhaps, be the fault of the Food and Drug Administration? Mr. Stetler has argued that FDA's cumbersome approval procedures are keeping wonderful new drugs off the market. He's disputed by an FDA official, Dr. John Jennings, who says that "until the federal government becomes as involved in drug research as we are in defense hardware . . . the drug industry and the drug industry alone must answer the question, 'Where are the new drugs?' "

Linus Pauling won two Nobel Prizes and should win another, if he has in fact discovered a cure for or learned how to prevent the common cold. Doctors fresh out of medical school gripe that they seldom see the esoteric diseases that really challenge diagnostic skills. What they see, day in and day out, are hypochondriacs—and people with the sniffles.

What if some wonderful day there were no colds? We could all rejoice. Doctors could do more important work if colds were passé.

But the transition would be difficult for the pharmaceutical companies, particularly the patent-medicine people who make millions, not curing colds or preventing them, but relieving symptoms, and not doing a very good job of that. Sales of aspirin, antihistamine, cough syrup, cough drops, lozenges, and mouth washes would drop drastically. The pharmaceutical companies' enthusiasm for a cold preventive would be very subdued, unless they held the patent on it.

Linus Pauling's cold preventive is vitamin C, which he says has never been recognized as having such properties because nobody ever took enough of it to do anything but avoid scurvy. The "minimum daily requirement" of vitamin C is small. By drinking orange juice or tomato juice or by popping One-a-Day vitamins one gets enough of it, but not enough to fend off the common cold. To prevent colds, he says, one must take at least two grams of vitamin C a day—eight big 250-milligram horse pills or half a teaspoon of vitamin C in powdered form. He believes the vitamin can also be used to cure a cold that's still in its first stages. To do that, he prescribes hourly doses of one gram for several hours till the cold vanishes.

I asked a proctologist friend of mine if massive doses of vitamin C such as Pauling suggests would be helpful. "It can't hurt," he said, somewhat contemptuously. He didn't care to discuss it further, possibly because colds are not his specialty and he'd heard enough of miracle cures that don't work. What my doctor said is correct, though it seems to damn Pauling with faint praise. Vitamin C is nontoxic and since the human system uses only what it needs and excretes the rest it doesn't build up in the body and cause problems, as taking too much vitamin A or D can.

But the medical profession is contemptuous of Dr. Pauling's cold remedy because, it is said, tests have never established that it works. *Time* magazine made that point when it said that Pauling had no evidence of a respectable sort that vitamin C wards off colds. *Time* didn't mention what Pauling does go into in his book, *Vitamin C and the Common Cold,* which is that experiments have never employed really large doses. It's therefore hardly surprising that the evidence has been negative or inconclusive.

Pauling's contention is that he has tried the cure and knows other people who have, and it works for him and them. That's the charm of the discovery. There's no need to take anybody's word on the subject as the truth. You can try it and discover for yourself. Either your cold rate will go down, perhaps to zero, or it won't. If it does, you'll need no endorsement from the American Medical Association, *Time* magazine, or the well-intentioned pharmaceutical companies, which continue to make money from preparations we all know aren't much help.

One caution: vitamin C, like all foods and drugs, *may* cause adverse reactions in certain persons and as a general rule self-prescription is a risky business. Deciding whether to take the cure or to wait until medical investigators spurred by Dr. Pauling verify his claims is a decision individuals will make for themselves. Vitamin C is freely available without prescription and is inexpensive, but caution may be prudent.

# 7
# politics in the marketplace

They may put a 16-inch gun on a canoe and attack somebody.

*Sears Roebuck Official*

Turn now to page 84 of the 1971 Sears Roebuck catalog for today's lesson in how to protect United States interests from the Communist threat. There you'll find a color illustration showing three little boats —a yellow canvas inflatable raft that comes in three sizes accommodating respectively three, four, or five adults; a green modified "semi-vee hull" gamefisher, twelve feet long and rated for three persons; and a pointed-stern aluminum canoe available in fifteen- and seventeen-foot models. The larger of the canoes has a maximum load capacity of 812 pounds. According to the catalog, all these boats have been reduced in price and are a bargain. But if you don't happen to be a citizen of the United States of America, the deal may be off. In the lower righthand corner of page 84 an "IMPORTANT NOTE" reads: "If you order a canoe or a gamefisher and are not a citizen of the United States, please state your country of origin." Catalog browsers may wonder what business it is of Sears where their customers were born and what possible bearing citizenship could have on buying a canoe.

I tried to find out from the Sears Roebuck general offices in Chicago. I first phoned a Mr. Ernest Arms, an information officer with the company. He didn't know anything about it but would "make every effort" to get to the bottom of it. Later, a Mr. Dan Fapp of Sears called back with the following information: "This is not the *legal* wording, but it is the essence of it. Apparently there's a U.S. Maritime Commission regulation that says boats—it does not specify what size—may not be sold to citizens of certain countries who do not have a special license. Most of the countries are those that you'd consider Iron Curtain countries—Cuba, Lithuania, Russia, and so forth. I understand that it's fairly easy to get one of these special licenses, but there are penalties if you sell a boat to a person without one."

Was the law passed to prevent anti-Castro Cubans from taking off from Miami in small boats to spark revolutions in Havana? "The law covers a multitude of countries," said Mr. Fapp. "I don't really know the historical background." Nor could he cite the specific law involved. "Since it is a U.S. Maritime Commission regulation, they would know," he said.

The Federal Maritime Commission (the U.S. Maritime Commission was abolished about twenty years ago) offered additional information. A lady in public information said when asked about the law, "I've never heard of such a thing. This agency wouldn't have anything to do with the sale of a canoe. We are a regulatory agency, but what we deal with are the big, oceangoing vessels in foreign trade or in domestic offshore trade." She turned me over to an attorney on the staff. "A law [that you can't sell boats to certain foreign nationals who don't have the United States government's permission] may apply perhaps to larger vessels, certainly not canoes, but in any event the agency involved there would be the U.S. Maritime *Administration,* not the Federal Maritime *Commission."* The Maritime Commission, the lawyer explained, regulates the foreign commerce industry. The Maritime Administration promotes the merchant marine and is also involved in subsidizing certain steamship companies. "I think in this instance what you are talking about may be one of the regulations of the Maritime Administration. It's located in the Commerce Department."

The man I was referred to at the Maritime Administration said he thought it "absurd" that anyone would be nervous about selling canoes to aliens. "Our agency is certainly not concerned with small craft. But there is a provision governing the sale of large vessels by American flag operators who want to dispose of their older ships. We have restrictions on the transfer of ships to Iron Curtain or Red Block countries. Normally they apply to naval vessels or ships that would have a wartime function. That would include merchant ships." But he doubted "pleasure boats" would come under such restrictions and promised to consult the Maritime Administration's general counsel.

The Maritime Administration's research disclosed that Sears' sales restriction is indeed rooted in law— Section 37 of the Shipping Act of 1916, which says that it is unlawful during a war or national emergency to sell any vessel to any alien without approval of the Maritime Administration. The United States has been and continues to be under a state of national emergency declared by President Truman on December 16, 1950.

Under regulations last revised in 1963 the provisions of the anachronistic Shipping Act have been eased somewhat. For instance, blanket approvals have been given to the sale of certain vessels to selected aliens. If a boat is under sixty-five feet in length, operates on less than six hundred horsepower, and displaces less than forty-five tons, it can be sold to any alien except those holding citizenship in the trade group known as the XYZ Countries, which currently include Hong Kong, Macao, Albania, Bulgaria, Czechoslovakia, East Germany, Estonia, Hungary, Latvia, Lithuania, Outer Mongolia, USSR, China (including Manchuria, but excluding Taiwan), North Korea, Communist-controlled areas of Vietnam, and Cuba. Any citizen from any of these countries—including a resident alien in the United States—must obtain permission to buy a seventeen-foot canoe. Sears Roebuck would make the necessary application for him, and the Maritime Administration would investigate it. One might think such applications were a rarity (the Boating Industries Association in Chicago, which represents manufacturers of sports boating equipment had never heard of any such restrictions on selling boats), but they do come up, particularly with Cubans resident in the United States. The spokesman for the Maritime Administration said he didn't know how many applications were received or what percentage of them were approved.

Politics stalks the marketplace in other ways. For instance, it has long been fashionable to avoid buying certain products that appear on idiosyncratic, homemade blacklists. Judy Bond clothes, Cat's Paw heels, Polish ham, Schick blades, Hunt's tomato paste,

Welch's candy, South African rock lobster, Supp-hose, California grapes, Volkswagens, and Saran Wrap have at one time or another been considered untouchable by some consumers, for good reason or bad.

Hunt Foods are on the personal boycott lists of some people who confuse the company name with H. L. Hunt. Actually, Mr. Hunt has nothing to do with Hunt foods. The food company is part of Norton Simon's conglomerate empire.

Welch candy was once an enterprise of Robert Welch of the John Birch Society, but he's no longer in the candy business. The grape juice Welch is "clean," although the company's former president, J. M. Kaplan, has a nonprofit foundation that several years ago acted as a conduit for the Central Intelligence Agency. California table grapes were on the list during a grape strike, but wine grapes from California were all right to buy. The Birch Society campaigned against Polish ham, denouncing it with bumper stickers that proclaimed that the ham is produced by "slave labor." Vestigial hatred of the Nazis turns some people off Volkswagens and other German imports.

It's hard to keep track of who's who on the boycott list, or when to take a product off the list, or what effect a personal boycott has. If boycotts affect corporate profits, one wouldn't know it from reading annual reports. Boycotts, unquestionably, are a nuisance, however. Hunt Foods, for instance, still has to send out hundreds of form letters disowning H. L. Hunt, and an executive of the company told me that he guessed the company lost a million dollars in business every year because of the mix-up in names.

The buyers-strike-to-end-the-war idea had a brief vogue among people who opposed the United States presence in Vietnam and were willing to make some small sacrifice to prove it. Strike proponents suggested that consumers cut back in their buying and go on a subsistence budget, purchasing only what they needed to live. More narrow lists were also proposed. A New Yorker by the name of Robert Rossner wrote several hundred friends, suggesting that they not buy things from companies thought to be especially influential with Richard Nixon. "If key industries felt that they were being hurt," he wrote, "they would use their considerable influence to bring an end to the war." Rossner singled out the airlines, electronics, telephones, plastics, and sugar. Postpone travel, he said, and whatever you do don't fly; make do with the home appliances you have; buy things packaged in glass, metal, or paper, but not plastic. Girls at Western College for Women in Oxford, Ohio, had as their slogan, "Stop Buying to Stop Dying." Their boycott list included products popular with students—beer and hard liquor, cosmetics, and records.

Boycott USA suggested buying imported goods rather than domestic products, using foreign banks and airlines, and buying gas from Shell (owned in part by the Netherlands). Specifically, they hoped people would stop patronizing the consumer products of the fifty top defense contractors; for example, Hertz rental cars (RCA), Remington shavers (Sperry Rand), Wonder Bread and Hostess cupcakes (International Telephone and Telegraph).

A buyers' strike is a very indirect method of influencing foreign policy, and such efforts seldom catch on. But they deserve respect as a legal, peaceful, personal expression of political feeling.


> You're living in the free world, in the free world you must stay.
>
> *Phil Ochs*

Some young people who find America increasingly hard to love are learning that it is not that easy to leave. Getting out of the country for a brief or extended stay requires more than impulse and a one-way ticket. If you are young, hippie in appearance, and without means, there is a chance that the country of your destination won't let you in. In evidence, I submit the case of a young couple, unmarried and nineteen, who flew to Glasgow. They had valid passports, friends waiting for them in Cambridge, and two hundred dollars cash. When their plane landed, they saw passengers in their thirties waved through customs perfunctorily, but they and other younger passengers were detained for special questioning. The interviews centered on whether they had return tickets or money enough to buy them. The couple did not, and as a result what money they had was confiscated and applied to the cost of a return ticket. They were put on the next flight back to New York.

A means test for tourists is not new, but there are indications that some countries, including the United States, have become fastidious in applying such a test selectively to young travelers whose appearance, behavior, and politics might be unconventional and who are suspected vagabonds. According to a U.S. State Department source, many nations now "do check to see if you have a way out. They fear that you may just end up a drifter and a public charge."

Persons inexperienced in international travel often make the mistake of thinking that a passport is all they need to enter a country and that they can get odd jobs to support themselves once there. Western European countries do not require United States citizens to obtain visas, under the assumption that a visit is what is intended. To get a job requires a work permit, obtained in advance from a foreign consulate. Entry to South American and Eastern European countries requires a visa. The United States itself has eighty different kinds of visas for foreign nationals planning trips here. Nonimmigrant visitors to the United States must usually have a return ticket, a ticket to another foreign point, or adequate funds to defray anticipated expenses. Immigration officers have discretionary authority to demand the posting of a departure bond.

Such policies seem rational. It's the arbitrariness of their application that's at question. According to a State Department official, the immigration service "has experienced a higher percentage of difficulty with the younger age groups. Our experience here is that Americans in the under-thirty group, shall we say, are those most likely to travel without money and with misinformation about the possibility of working abroad." Oddly enough, the State Department has isolated the problem, but has made no efforts to warn citizens before they leave the country.

A British consular officer in Washington believes that the United Kingdom's refusal to admit tourists without return passage needs no defense, nor does he think it particularly remarkable that customs officials in Glasgow and elsewhere employ stereotypes in the exercise of their discretion. "It's fairly obvious that a person who is obviously well-heeled would have the means to return to the United States," he said, so he might not be asked questions. Young freaks, on the other hand, are something else, though he agrees that stereotyping travelers by looks or age may be unfair.

According to the British official, international airlines are skittish about selling one-way tickets, since it is they who sometimes must foot the bill for the return of a passenger refused entry. However, John Corris, in public relations for Trans World Airways (TWA), thinks it extraordinary that anyone would ask a passenger if he has a return ticket or how much money he has. Certainly TWA doesn't. "Our basic responsibility is to deliver a passenger who buys a ticket from point A to point B. There have been occasions where a government has refused to admit a person as undesirable either because he is a criminal or for political reasons. It then becomes the responsibility of the airline to take him someplace else." A passenger with a one-way ticket and no money at all would, if refused entry, also be returned by TWA at the company's expense. Pan American assumes similar responsibility, invoking it most often in cases in which a tourist somehow manages to get aboard a flight with a ticket but without a passport. If he can't obtain one after deplaning in Europe he is returned home free. Neither TWA nor Pan Am seems to have any qualms about selling one-way tickets.

It is impossible to tell how many poor, young, hairy, radical, pot-smoking, potential drones on foreign states are sent home, since no one keeps the statistics. But seasoned travelers are surprised that it happens at all. *They* have never been asked to reveal the contents of their wallets or ticket folders. Clark Winter, an American Express official in New York who has "traveled a great deal, claims that all he has ever had to do is to fill out a visitor's entry card with his name, address, passport number, and such. "To my recollection, no one has ever asked me if I had a round-trip ticket." But then Winter presumably looks respectable. Traditionally, United States and other embassies throughout the world have provisions for what are called "distressed subjects." If he encounters financial difficulties abroad, one can go for help to the embassy of his nation. However, that relief is no longer considered sufficient protection by nations wary of alienated, alien youth.

# 8
# nothing works anymore
## ... and you can't fix it

The technology responsible for our great American conveniences has an associated disadvantage; each mechanical moving part can stop working. There are more machines to break down than ever (55 million vacuum cleaners alone), and the social mechanisms for producing, selling, and servicing the technology don't work well either. The machinery has become more complicated, in the process all but eliminating the handyman, the fix-it shop, and do-it-yourself attempts. (You can't tinker with a printed circuit.) The pressures of competition in a market economy invite a cheapening of materials. (The foil wears off the chrome trim, revealing the plastic.) Here the con game is played with abandon. Products are meant to wear out so they will have to be replaced. Parts are priced so as to make it more economical to replace than to repair. The inducements and status of service jobs have declined so far that there is little pride, less competence, and no money in the work. (The country is short seventy thousand auto mechanics.)

Several congressmen, ladies at the White House, government regulators, and a growing number of reporters are making careers out of exploring the distress people feel when the machines in their lives break down. The impression that everything is going to hell may be, in part, a creature of the coverage. The conviction that things *were* better and lasted longer years ago may be written off as nostalgia. Consumer-oriented politicians may be suspected of *creating* issues for votes. But when one January morning you try to call the New York City Housing Administration to complain that you're cold and that the furnace in your building has collapsed, and you can't get through because your phone isn't working either, then you know it's not make-believe. Nothing *does* work. For instance, it is a simple fact that if machines could be trusted and, failing that, if repairmen were reliable, it would not be necessary for Allen Funt, despite all the money he made producing Candid Camera, to have in his kitchen two ovens, two stoves, two refrigerators, and two freezers. "I've always lived in homes where things break down," Funt told a newspaper interviewer. "When you have two of everything, one is bound to work."

Malfunction knows no bounds. The first commercial flight of the hyperthyroid Boeing 747 jet was seven hours late because an engine overheated and a door jammed, so passengers had to be transferred to a standby plane. The engines, operating at low thrust so as to avoid exhaust damage to the airport, were incapacitated by wind. It was the third major flaw discovered in the Pratt and Whitney engines. (They should have known there'd be trouble when Pat Nixon christened the plane with a machine spraying red, white, and blue water that wouldn't turn off on cue.)

The very week in which the Metroliner, Penn Central's experimental fast train between Washington, D.C. and New York, celebrated its first year "in service," half the scheduled six daily runs had to be canceled because parts froze. Even when conditions are optimal, only six of the originally anticipated nine trains are in service because equipment is not performing properly. Men at the Budd Company would like to redesign the trains in less of a hurry, so that the bugs could be worked out. Passengers have noticed that mechanisms on some reclining seats are broken. Random overhead lights are out. Doors between cars, built to be opened automatically at the touch of a hand, must be pried open.

Fifteen percent of New York's subway trains regularly run late, thus delaying six hundred thousand passengers daily. The chairman of the Transit Authority admits service has deteriorated, but he says that despite a fare increase there won't be money to service the trains properly for quite some time. Passengers complain that they must stand in idle trains for up to an hour while the trains stall, doors refuse to close, power fails, or switches stick.

An inch of snow and a sluggish city snow removal service one winter day in Washington, D.C., brought to mind the old Michael Rennie movie *The Day the Earth Stood Still*. The streets became a parking lot. Senator William Proxmire, who often jogged to work in forty-five minutes, was trapped in a car for twice the time. A fifteen-minute drive home took two to three hours. The same day, and on cold January mornings, the D.C. Transit System of buses was forced to cancel part of its rush-hour service because of frozen air lines that kept brakes and doors from working. Antifreeze chemicals in Washington are discovered only after they are needed.

With buses, trains, and planes operating on hit-or-miss schedules, in good weather one can sometimes drive —*if* the car is working. Senator Philip Hart concluded from hearings he held on automobile repairs that a third of all repairs are unsatisfactory and that nine out of ten cars more than five years old have things wrong with them that pertain to safety. This is true, despite the fact that Americans spent $8.8 billion on repairs in 1969 ($138 for each of the 64 million cars). Hart received six thousand letters from persons with car-repair horror stories. He figured that for each letter there were probably a thousand unreported incidents.

What is true of transportation is true of communication. One no longer can be sure that a busy signal means the phone is in use. The circuits may be overloaded, or the press on the Bell System's deficient personnel and equipment too great. In New York, where the problems appear most severe, the Public Service Commission received in the first half of 1969 more than forty-three hundred complaints about phone service. That October the city's Parks Administration complained that it had not been able to make outgoing calls since July. Turnover among New York telephone operators is about 60 percent. The result is lower hiring standards and thicker-witted operators, who, if you get them, either don't understand what you've said or dial a wrong number.

If you can't phone, try writing a letter. *Life* magazine sent thirty-five hundred letters to and from twenty-two cities to test the Post Office. It found that a letter from

Seattle, with airmail stamp, zip code, and the rest, took nine days to reach Washington, D.C.

What Ronald Reagan said about redwoods and Spiro Agnew said about slums is certainly true of the letters Mrs. Virginia Knauer got as the White House Special Assistant for Consumer Affairs. The laments were endless—a sudden, unannounced reduction in voltage, damaging appliances; potholes in (recently paved) streets; overflowing sewers; new tires that blow out; paint that peels; plaster that cracks. Two thousand letters each month complained about products and services, and, when you've read one, you've read them all. They adhere to an instinctive and universal form that goes approximately as follows:

> On a specific date I bought a particular product at a certain store. It either didn't work from the start or soon broke down, and when I took it back or called in the store's serviceman, they either couldn't or wouldn't fix it, or after they had fixed it it still didn't work. The warranty was not honored [had just expired, or did not cover the necessary repair]. The store would not stand back of its merchandise, and letters to the manufacturer accomplished nothing.

I thought it would be interesting to spend a few hours in Mrs. Knauer's office, the pinched-nerve center of all our complaints. After that, it was easy to understand why someone in the business of receiving desperate, intemperate, bitchy, and humorless communications (delayed) might become cynical or at least impervious. A man who has written five letters threatens to go to court over a $3.72 misunderstanding; an apparently well-to-do businessman buys Ford's "most expensive and most elegant" auto, the Thunderbird, only to find that for all his money he's gotten a lemon; and a woman finds that the Good Housekeeping guarantee is only as good as her own ability to provide conclusive evidence that the salesman misled her about the properties of her vacuum cleaner.

As predictable as most letters are in their anger, some still have the power to move; for example this, from Florida:

> My husband and I are retired. He is 76 years old and has had a stroke. I am 70. I thought we could enjoy a color set since he stays in quite a lot. I paid near $700.00 for the television and antenna. They have worked on the set about nine times and it still don't give good service. They are supposed to have a district area man to come around once in a while to check on televisions but so far they haven't brought him by to check on ours. I have asked them when he would be in this area but the answer is they don't know. There was a three months' warranty on the set and they were called four times in the three months. Each time I told them I wanted it fixed or a new set. Each time they said they had fixed it and they were sure it would be ok. They have made nine service calls already. I went to see them again this month and they said they were waiting for the area man to come around. I just don't believe they intend doing anything about it. I don't feel like I can afford to hire a lawyer and take it to court. I certainly would appreciate any help you can give us. For we need it.

Mrs. Knauer, whose limits perfectly symbolize the government's commitment, replied that she truly sympathized and was sorry she didn't have the power to help. In her first year in office Mrs. Knauer did not have the authority from the President to do anything but reply in a friendly way to consumer complaints. "The letters we sent were horrendous," said one of Mrs. Knauer's ghosts. "It was a policy of the runaround," according to another. Paragraph one of a typical Knauer letter summarized the consumer's complaint. ("Thank you for your recent letter concerning your controversy with the dealer over the insurance received when your television receiver was struck by lightning and subsequent difficulties you are experiencing in obtaining service to the replacement set.") Paragraph two commiserated and explained the role of the President's consumer advisor. ("As sympathetic as I am with your problems, I must honestly report that the powers of my office do not include intervention in a controversy between buyer and seller for purposes of adjustment.") Finally, the letter offered an appropriate homily or suggestion for redress, usually in the form of a referral to another agency. The referral might be to the Federal Trade Commission, a state attorney-general or consumer office, or to an industry group like the National Association of Automobile Dealers. The strongest encouragement came when the consumer seemed to be handling his problem himself and didn't need Mrs. Knauer: "I heartily endorse your action in letting the manufacturer know of your dissatisfaction," or "There is no better substitute to securing adjustment to consumer service problems than the direct action by the consumer himself."

Letters responding to complaints forwarded to the White House by members of Congress were longer, more thorough. Letters from lunatics, nasty letters, and flippant letters didn't get answered at all. Thus a letter that began, "I am nominating the Gibson Refrigerator

Company for the Flying Fickle Finger of Fate award," had a notation at the top: "Letter abusive to manufacturer, no reply sent."

In December 1969 Mrs. Knauer's office was told that it could begin interceding in small ways with manufacturers. She now could forward letters of complaint to the companies cited. About twice a day someone in Mrs. Knauer's office would telephone a company to see if something could be done to get one unhappy person what he wanted. Mrs. Knauer kept a success file, which included the few cases in which a phone call or a letter from her office accomplished something for somebody. In a country of 20,721,390 electric can-openers, that's not much.

Joseph Dawson, the Public Affairs Director of the President's Office of Consumer Affairs and a member of Mrs. Knauer's staff, refuses to be disheartened. Within thirty years, he believes, the "various forces" that are trying to assist consumers will have prevailed, and those of us still here will be living in a "quality society." Color television sets presumably will not catch fire. "The problem then will be understanding why we still aren't happy." Meanwhile, however, the problem is a simpler one: Why aren't we efficient?

Consider the American Automobile Association (AAA); if you're a member, you're entitled to free emergency road service. In the city a call to AAA gets a flat tire changed or a dead battery back to life within fifteen to forty-five minutes, depending on traffic, weather conditions, and such. It's a useful service, certainly, and to my mind well worth the fifteen to twenty-three dollars' membership fee (rates differ from place to place; they're higher in New York, for example, than in Macon, Georgia). According to John Eck, director of AAA's emergency road service program, AAA answers 11 million calls each year for its 12 million members. AAA has under contract twenty-six thousand service stations and garages, many with radio-dispatched trucks. The service you get seems as good as the fellow who answers the call.

I make use of AAA emergency service several times a year and have over the years gotten service that's hard to fault, with one exception worth discussing because it says something about the service and repair business generally. It is almost an axiom: Service is great when a guy's got something to sell you, but it's terrible when you want him to take something back.

One February night my battery konked out in a bad neighborhood. I phoned AAA, which quickly dispatched a service vehicle. After attaching his jumper cables to my battery and giving me five seconds to attempt ignition, the service man gave up the effort. The battery could not be charged, he said, and he refused to give it a second try. He didn't test the battery with a hydrometer; he didn't check the alternator. The battery, he insisted, was shot.

I had two alternatives: to buy a new battery from him (of course, he had one with him) or to leave my car stranded. It wasn't a difficult choice, even though the AAA Club battery (made for AAA by Gould-National Batteries, Inc.) cost $32.00, which was more than I was eager to spend and a lot more than I might have had to spend had I been able to shop around. (I've priced some that run as little as $19.95.) But I was a captive customer, and I bought.

The Club battery was guaranteed for forty-eight months and the service man assured me that it was a first-quality battery, not cheap in either sense of the word. It worked very well for six months; then it seemed that every time I tried to start my car I had to ring up AAA. The guy who answered my first call started the car, but advised me to proceed directly to a service station to get the battery charged and the terminals cleaned of accumulated corrosion (a major cause of battery failure). I did. When I picked up the car, I was told my battery was defective. The post that extends down into the battery from one of the terminals was loose. I should take the battery back to wherever I had purchased it.

I didn't follow that advice immediately, since the car ran all right, but a week later the battery went dead again—in the morning as I left home for work, at noon when I went to lunch, and at night when I left my office. Exasperated, I phoned the AAA Office of Emergency Road Service for instructions about where to take my "defective" battery. It was then I learned that, although you can buy a battery from the guy who answers your service call, you can't take it back to him when you want to invoke the guarantee. Nor will AAA send someone out to check the battery and replace it under the guarantee. For that (in Washington, D.C.) one must drive many miles to an AAA-leased service station in the Maryland suburbs.

When I arrived at that Maryland service station the same evening, I was told by the attendant that he couldn't do anything for me. He was baffled that AAA had sent me to him. Moreover, his testing equipment was locked up for the night. He couldn't give me a new battery. I would have to come back the next morning —a Saturday—or, better yet, some weekday.

I was glad, in a perverse way, that when I attempted to drive away mad, I couldn't start the car. Neither could the reluctant mechanic. He tried jumper cables; he tried polishing the terminals to a metallic shine. The engine would not turn over. The circumstances were identical to those the previous February, when I had bought the battery under duress; the battery wouldn't take a charge. But whereas in February AAA was eager to replace my battery with a new and expensive one, in October there was no such accommodating impulse—no new battery, period. After an hour of attempting, and failing in the attempt, to juice up the battery, the car finally started, and I drove away promising to return the next morning to speak with the station manager.

Needless to say, I had to phone AAA to start my car the next morning. In a long—and by this time emotional—phone conversation I related the history of my battery and tried to prevail upon the road service man, and then his supervisor, to send me out a new battery. The supervisor heard me out and implied he'd do something, but the man in the tow truck said he wasn't authorized to make good AAA's guarantee. He had no trouble starting my car.

The manager of AAA's suburban filling station couldn't understand why I had gotten no satisfaction the night before. The attendant, he said, "just didn't want to get his hands dirty." The manager checked the battery, checked the alternator, explained to me that the battery was not defective (the posts in AAA's new-fangled plastic batteries are all loose!), isolated a problem in the alternator, charged the battery, charged me three dollars, and sent me off with a functioning automobile. So the AAA battery was not defective! But no matter —the service I had got *was* deficient.

Virginia Knauer has had more complaints about car trouble than anything else. I would bet, therefore, that my experience was no fluke. At moments of such minor crises one is prone to generalized, and possibly unreasonable, conclusions: sellers have no interest in the quality or durability of their products and no abiding commitment to their guarantees; service men are desultory and incompetent; everything is going to hell.

Less than a year and a half ago I bought four new tires at Sears to replace the baldies on my old Mustang. They had, after two years, become too dangerous to drive on. The new Sears tires were moderately priced sale tires, guaranteed to last three years. I didn't read the guarantee carefully, I simply assumed that the tires would last for some specified period or that they would be replaced.

*Guarantee* is a magic word of salesmanship. Although it has no fixed meaning, it has always implied to me that a product will work as advertised or the store (possibly the manufacturer) will make it good. Guarantees generally are so baroquely worded that customers —and salesmen eager to clinch the sale—usually make do with such simplistic definitions, even if they often turn out to be wrong. In the case of my tires, things didn't work out as I had expected, though I can hardly blame Sears for my not reading the guarantee.

I'm not at ease in a tire store. For one thing, I never know which tires to buy, and I'm not alone. *Consumer Reports,* in its annual *Buying Guide,* warns that "you cannot consistently count on any single type of construction or material to give better performance than another." Newspaper ads for tires always make it seem that whether you buy a cheap tire or an expensive one, one that's used, new, or recapped, you're getting a good tire. You expect, if you have good sense, that a more expensive tire will last longer and be safer, but you can't be sure of that. What seems to be more expensive may not in the long run *be* more expensive. According to *Consumer Reports,* you can spend $183 for four tires with an estimated tread life of forty thousand miles and spend in effect only $46 per ten thousand driving miles. Or you can buy cheapo tires with an expected life of fifteen thousand miles for $107 at an average cost of $71 per ten thousand miles.

Ralph Nader launched his career exposing unsafe tires. The Federal Trade Commission charged Firestone with deceptive pricing and savings claims and with misrepresenting the quality of its products. Bad news about tires worries me; bad tires can get you killed.

Changing to snow tires in the fall and taking them off in the spring always seems to take a full day. Since I'm not mechanically inclined, I take my car back to Sears (where I also bought snow tires) because they don't charge anything for changing tires they've sold. But oh, the agony of waiting in line. I now know better than to go late in the fall, or when snow is predicted, or on the first nice spring day. But no matter when I go, there is always a line measurable in hours of idleness. My reason tells me it's impossible, yet I come away convinced that most Sears mechanics are always at lunch.

I bought relatively expensive tires because I thought it would mean that I wouldn't have to go back to Sears (save for my seminannual tire change) for thirty-six months. Little more than a year later, the tires were worthless. One was bald, another had an aneurysm ready to rupture, and a third had a not-so-slow leak that necessitated daily inflating. There wasn't much to collect, for my three-year guarantee entitled me to only a 20 percent trade-in allowance on the purchase of new tires. Some guarantee; in addition to the meager reduction on new tires, it ensured that for the foreseeable future I would remain in the clutches of Sears.

Had I expected too much of the guarantee? A federal task force on appliance warranties, initiated in the Johnson Administration, recommended that, among other things, warranties should be worded simply and should recognize that "the purchaser . . . is entitled to receive a product which is reasonably suitable for the purpose for which it is intended." It also recommended that manufacturers "not attempt to pass on to the consumer . . . a part or all of the financial burden of replacing defective parts or of correcting defects in design or manufacture."

The Senate in August 1970 passed a bill which, while not requiring anybody to guarantee any product, set guidelines for guarantees and warranties that *are* offered. It required simple English. It obligated manufacturers offering "full warranties" to replace or repair malfunctioning or defective products within a "reasonable" time after purchase. And it forbade manufacturers to disown responsibility for the proper functioning of products. I take this to mean that tires guaranteed for thirty-six months should last thirty-six months, at the very least.

The tread wear-out guarantee that came with my Sears Allstate tires was, I concede, simply worded. But it was no source of joy. I had bought tires, expecting them to last three years, and after little more than one I had to buy new tires at Sears with nothing but a small discount to console me. I acquiesced, not knowing what else to do.

This time, armed with the latest *Consumer Reports Buying Guide* I could find, I decided to buy the very best tires available—Sears steel Radials—tires that would still be good long after my car had turned to junk. Consumer's Union rates Sears Radials second only to Michelin X, a French tire which everyone assured me is the best you can buy. Indeed, Sears Radials are made by Michelin too. The tread design is different, but Michelin, company spokesmen say, makes only one grade of tires. The *Buying Guide* said that Radials last for forty thousand miles; have average stopping distance capability, well above average rupture resistance, and average traction; and cost only forty-seven dollars per ten thousand miles. They'd be a good buy, I thought.

But Sears, which advertises the tires, didn't have any. It didn't have any, the salesman (who kept me coming back every day for a week on the promise that "they'll be in this afternoon") told me, because of "the tire strike." A strike by four thousand rubber workers at Armstrong Rubber Company, Sears' supplier, had reduced shipments to a trickle, he said, and, unless the strike was settled soon, there'd be no one in Sears' tire department to receive my complaints.

Since I had been planning a car trip and saw in this predicament a chance to get out of Sears' grasp, I called a branch of Market Tire Company, a national chain that handles Michelin, which advertised "sizes to fit most American cars" and "over 50,000 tires in stock at all times." The explanation I got this time was not "the tire strike," but "an import ban" that had been imposed on tires. Michelin could not be imported from France, the salesman told me, and, until Michelin's Canadian factory went into operation the next year, the supply of Michelins would be scant to nil. It seemed pointless for Market Tire to continue to advertise products it no longer had in stock.

When I phoned Armstrong in Connecticut, I was told that tire shipments had continued during the strike and that there should have been no shortage of tires supplied by the company. Then a Michelin spokesman in Lake Success, New York, informed me that there was no import ban; there was going to be a new plant in Canada, he said, but the national shortage of Michelin tires was the result of demand. Michelins for American cars have been available only since early 1967, and sales have increased dramatically. United States sales run to more than a million tires annually. Michelin can't keep up with sales. In the meantime I wanted to drive to Colorado and couldn't on my three-year, guaranteed tires, dead before their time.

I did finally get my tires and, wallet bursting with credit cards, made the trip. Some people collect coins; I collect credit cards. It gives me a feeling of security to know that simply by signing my name I can quickly and painlessly put myself in debt. Currently I have twelve plastic cards (not counting duplicates), including five oil company cards, three department store cards, one airline card, and three of the so-called prestige cards for which one must pay an annual membership charge —American Express and *two* Diners Club cards, one for business and one for personal use.

I applied for all of them—nobody has ever sent me an unsolicited credit card—and I have been given all the cards I applied for, with one exception. I was turned down by BankAmericard. I wanted a BankAmericard for my collection and also because, to quote the brochure, "it's the most versatile credit card you can carry." Unlike American Express, BankAmericard does not require that cardholders pay their entire statement balance each month. They can opt instead for small monthly payments and the legal usury of 18 percent interest. BankAmericard carriers can borrow money (up to five hundred dollars) by presenting their card at a participating bank. The best American Express will do for you is to cash your checks (up to fifty dollars) at any American Express office. No doubt, American Express has its advantages over BankAmericard; perhaps more restaurants in more parts of the world honor it. I thought BankAmericard could do something for me, however, and I wanted to be one of the millions of BankAmericard cardholders. But it was not in the cards for me.

I had filled out the application "completely and correctly" according to the instructions, disclosing such information as the amounts and sources of my income, my rent, where I work, and my marital status. Perhaps the BankAmericard folks found something in this biographical data that worried them. I'll not defend my credit record, except to say that I pay my bills and I have all those other credit cards. Whatever the credit bureaus have turned up that might affect my credit rating hasn't kept me from getting credit wherever I have asked for it.

My first communication from BankAmericard was a form letter I found annoying and uninformative:

> *Dear Mr. Sanford:*
> Saying "yes" is easy and enjoyable. Saying "no" is a most unhappy experience for us. Unfortunately, after a thorough and confidential review of your application for BankAmericard, it has been disapproved. Your interest in BankAmericard is appreciated, and we truly regret not being able to accommodate you. For your protection, your application will be destroyed.
> Sincerely,
> *E. C. Smith, Credit Manager*
> *United Virginia*
> *BankAmericard Center*

I wanted to know more, so I wrote Paul E. Sackett, the president of United Virginia Bank. I told him who I was and explained, "I am writing to you because I assume Mr. E. C. Smith is a credit-office conceit, not a real person, and that should I contact your credit office I would merely receive another form letter. . . . I would like to ask you, as a personal favor, to (1) see that my application receives careful reexamination and (2) explain to me how it is that your credit office failed to approve my application. . . . I am distressed to think that my credit rating has been blackened for reasons I have no knowledge of." I sent a copy to E. C. Smith, in case he was real.

Mr. Sackett replied promptly that he did not have jurisdiction over my problem but that he had forwarded my letter to someone who did and that he hoped things would work out satisfactorily. Soon thereafter I got a letter from William T. Hunt, another "Credit Manager," who told me that my "request for reconsideration has been forwarded to Mr. L. A. Deppenbrock of the United Virginia Bank of Fairfax, the bank who originally reviewed your application. Please allow time for your application to reach Mr. Deppenbrock by mail, and then he will contact you regarding his decision." The letter was the last I heard from my friends at BankAmericard.

Now many months later I am still curious why I am persona non grata to BankAmericard, although I am less eager to do business with them. Under the Federal Fair Credit Reporting Act, effective April 25, 1971, BankAmericard cannot brush people off so easily. The law requires a company, when it rejects an applicant for credit, to disclose in the same letter the name and address of the credit bureau on whose information the company based its decision. The applicant then has the right to go to the credit bureau and inspect the information sold to BankAmericard. If the information is erroneous, it can be corrected. The applicant can demand a reinvestigation of disputed information in his file. Or, as a last resort, he can prepare a concise statement, giving his own explanation or rebuttal of the disputed data. It then becomes a part of the file and must be sent to anyone who buys information from the credit bureau in the future.

I'm not sure I know what generalizations one might draw from my experiences with Sears, AAA, and BankAmericard, except perhaps that they are not unique and that "consuming" is becoming a full-time job.

# 9
# fighting
# back

If one had to pick a date for the renaissance of the muckracking consumer movement in this country, March 1966 would be a defensible choice. For it was in that month that James Roche, then the president of General Motors, apologized publicly to Ralph Nader for putting private detectives on his tail. The detectives had been asking Nader's friends unseemly questions about his private life in the apparent hope that they'd find out something to shut him up about the Corvair. That episode cost GM far more than the six thousand dollars it paid for the services of Vincent Gillen, the private detective. First was Roche's ordeal, experienced under hot television lights in a Capitol hearing room filled with spectators and members of the Senate. (Robert Kennedy was on the committee. Ted Sorensen, the Kennedy family friend, was there as one of Roche's lawyers.) Then came the death of the Corvair, whose sales had dropped off precipitously. And don't forget the settlement of more than four-hundred thousand dollars GM worked out with Nader to get him to drop his invasion-of-privacy suit.

It's hard to believe, but until that day in 1966 Ralph Nader was not well known and the consumer movement didn't amount to much. Nader owes a lot to General Motors, though it's a debt neither would be eager to acknowledge. Nader's reputation is now firmly based on his own achievements, and GM and James Roche, the retired chairman of the General Motors Corporation, are still resisting the movement Nader leads.

In the years since GM's humiliation, many corporations have decided, at least for purposes of good public relations, to join the consumer movement. The Philco division of the Ford Motor Company, for instance, wrote consumer reporters, hoping to get some publicity for its stated efforts in behalf of the consumer: "We would like you to know that Philco-Ford stands ready in any way it can to help you meet the challenge of consumer reporting," the letter began.

> Our company would be pleased to help you answer general or specific questions about the products we manufacture and sell—TV sets, radios, stereos, refrigerator-freezers and air conditioners. Philco-Ford was the first in its industry to appoint a high level executive to the position of consumer affairs vice president. We think consumerism is good business. Naturally, we can't help your readers if they experience a service problem with another brand product, but we can with ours. More importantly, we can also help if readers want to know how to buy appliances or electronics products, how to use them or care for them. Please do not hesitate to call on us if we can in any way help you or your readers.

Although consumer writers might be put off by such blatant self-promotion as Philco-Ford's, it does take a certain amount of bravery to declare yourself proconsumer. To do so makes a company vulnerable when consumers can prove from their own experience that the company's claims are so much baloney. The automotive division of Ford pictures itself in television advertising as "talking straight" to consumers, telling them the truth about the quality of cars, about pollution, and about value.

The Senate Commerce Subcommittee at one point toyed with holding hearings for the purpose of congratulating certain firms—namely, Sears, Motorola, Whirlpool, and Quaker Oats—for their efforts in behalf of consumers. The subcommittee's chairman, Frank Moss of Utah, said, "In our zeal to strike back at [irresponsible behavior among several of the largest corporations] we have not given sufficient credit to those companies which have displayed an uncommon sense of responsibility."

Not everyone would agree who the "responsible" corporations are. (Moss, for instance, thinks Ford, as well as General Motors, has been irresponsible in exaggerating the costs of auto safety improvements.) But unquestionably there is merit in giving credit to those corporations and businesses that are interested in more than making money—that have an interest in the quality, durability, and satisfactory servicing of their products, in truthful advertising, in equity in the marketplace, and in reasonable consumer legislation.

Unlike Ford and a few other companies, General Motors has continued to take a hard line against "consumerism," viewing it as more of a menace than a boon to corporations. In a speech to the Executive Club of Chicago, GM chairman Mr. Roche said:

Individuals and agencies have competed—
sometimes blindly—to be on the crest of the wave
of consumer protection. In the 1960s, consumer
legislation came into political vogue. Much of this
was necessary, and serves our society well. Yet
the short-term political advantage offered by spec-
tacular but unsound consumer legislation can do
lasting damage to the very consumers it purports
to help.

The consumer is the loser when irresponsible criticism and ill-conceived legislation break down
faith in our economic system, when harassment
distracts us from our modern challenges, when the
very idea of free enterprise is diminished in the
eyes of the young people who must one day man-
age our businesses.

Corporate responsibility is a catchword of the ad-
versary culture that is so evident today. If something is wrong with American society, blame
business.

The dull cloud of pessimism and distrust which
some have cast over free enterprise is impairing
the ability of business to meet its basic economic
responsibilities. . . . This, as much as any other
factor, makes it urgent that those of us who are in
business stand up and be counted.

Corporation executives like Mr. Roche, usually so conscious of where their interests lie, can be remarkably
forgetful of the source of their six-figure salaries. Consumers are the people who buy (or don't buy) what
they sell. In the image-making business, Ford has the
better idea.

Virginia Knauer has had the idea that we'd all be better off if there were more consumer education in the

schools. What for? Well, for one thing, to teach kids that "possessions cannot bring complete happiness." Education of the sort Mrs. Knauer envisions would also teach that machines are extraordinarily complicated, that products are baffling in their variety, and that salesmen are sometimes—how shall we put it— devious.

The increasing complexity and variety of commercial malpractice is a logical justification for consumer education, but can the schools teach defenses against all the offenses of the world? If every difficult social problem were to spawn a high school class in "coping," the schools would proliferate in karate, marksmanship, antidotes, and armorplate. The emphasis and the effort just might be misplaced. Should children have to take, as Mrs. Knauer has recommended, "courses in tactics of used car salesmen," or might it not be better to make car dealers take courses in simple honesty?

Government—particularly the regulatory agencies— has a role in enforcing fair business practices on sellers, and the schools have a responsibility to teach buyers how to behave. Intelligent consuming—"buymanship" in the parlance of consumer educators— would make the marketing system more responsive and responsible. That is, if the consumer knows what he is doing, he won't be as easily done in. And businessmen will have to try new and, presumably, more forthright selling approaches.

Yet there is something cynical about consumer education proposals coming from government officials, since the federal government has done so little either to legislate consumer protection or to educate consumers.

For many years the Veterans Administration, which had carried out extensive laboratory research on hearing aids, wouldn't release to the public its test results on the grounds that doing so would give unfair competitive advantage to the companies that made the best products.

I'm not suggesting the federal government has been oblivious to consumer interests. The *Suggested Guidelines for Consumer Education* published by the President's Committee on Consumer Interests is useful, and suitably broad to allow teachers to stress what they will. Here and there within the syllabus there is room for the teacher to criticize government, industry, and the cherished values of materialism and consumption.

Nevertheless, many of the resources suggested by the *Guidelines* are biased in favor of the unmonitored marketplace. For instance, it is suggested that fourth-graders be asked to "list the ways in which insurance helps people in personal financial losses." And it is proposed that an insurance agent be invited to school to discuss with seventh-graders "factors that determine insurance costs." You wouldn't expect the kids to learn from such experiences anything about loopholes in coverage, fine-print insurance contracts, and the difficulty old people have in obtaining, even at a high cost, life and health insurance. Nor would you expect them to hear about auto insurers who cancel policies after an accident or about how insurance companies have lobbied state legislatures to let them set their own excessive rates. The children will learn these things if the teacher is on the ball, but only then.

"Consumer education," Mrs. Knauer has said, "is an imperative need for every young person in America."

Who can disagree? But in a world without price fixing, collusion, restraint of trade, slack filling, packaging to price, bait and switch, dangling comparatives, and other ingenious and baffling marketplace devices, "buymanship" wouldn't be essential. Even in a corrupted marketplace it isn't all that helpful; knowing how the marketplace works doesn't mean you won't become its victim anyway. ✗

How does one become a "better buyer," knowing there are certain consumer problems that are almost impossible to solve short of going to court? Legal action is too complicated and expensive a way to get satisfaction, especially when the financial stakes are small.

For example, what does a customer do when he has bought a piece of furniture that is defective, and the salesman refuses to do anything about it? He can gripe, but too often "complaint departments" that exist to handle dissatisfied customers offer no more than vague and worthless promises. The customer can go over the merchant's head and write the Federal Trade Commission, the White House, and the local Better Business Bureau. But what can and what will they do? Public agencies are swamped with complaints; they are understaffed, lacking in statutory powers, and slow even if they are interested in your problem. Better Business Bureaus are associations of businessmen, not consumers, and their bias is that of the merchant. There *is* one recourse that is almost sure to get action —not necessarily favorable, but action nevertheless. You can picket.

I know someone who tried for four months to get the New York furniture store, W & J Sloane, Inc., to take care of a small imperfection in a corduroy seat cover. It was admittedly no big problem, but the customer service department at Sloane's turned a deaf ear to the complaint. The customer stewed and as he did, the corduroy seat cover became a matter of principle. So one morning he bought a sandwich-board placard on which he lettered "Sloane's stuck me with defective furniture." He put the placard on his back and paced back and forth in front of the Fifth Avenue store. He had a hunch that Sloane's would not like this sort of "grass roots publicity."

He was right. In an hour in front of the store he was approached by twenty-one passersby who wanted to wish him well, give him advice, or tell him about their own consumer problems with big stores. After he'd been picketing for five minutes, a Sloane's floorwalker asked him to come inside for a chat with the store manager. He refused. Five minutes later the manager himself appeared to invite him in to speak with the executive vice-president. My friend again refused, explaining that, whatever happened, he intended to continue his protest demonstration for at least one hour. Afterwards he would be glad to go inside. After the hour he entered the store to see Jack P. Donis, the executive vice-president. Donis was all cordiality. He apologized for the defective merchandise and for the performance of the customer service department (it's hard to get good help); he immediately saw to it that the seat cover in question was replaced to the customer's satisfaction.

Mr. Donis kept the placard in his office for several weeks after the incident and wore it to a meeting of Sloane's customer service group where, according to

Donis, it was greeted with "total shock and dismay." He hoped his own little demonstration would embarrass his people into performing better for customers. Later he wrote the customer that he was sorry that "we drove you to the extremes we did" and that "hopefully you have performed a service for all Sloane customers." Mr. Donis behaved like a champ, perhaps because the picketing scene was a genuine embarrassment of the kind a responsible and respected business would like to discourage.

Picketing is an effective ploy for consumers, if, that is, they can avoid certain pitfalls, such as suits for libel or court injunctions.

Ralph Nader, Lowell Dodge, and Ralf Hotchkiss are the authors of *What to Do with Your Bad Car.* In it are contained 175 pages of useful suggestions for protecting one's rights as the buyer of a new or used car. For drivers who aren't mechanically inclined, the book is far more helpful than the maintenance manual the dealer supplies, for it tells how you can get someone else to fix your car, hopefully at his expense rather than yours. The book has chapters on the basic mechanics of a car; the most frequent breakdowns, the provisions of the customary warranty and a model warranty which would offer more protection from the buyer's standpoint; suggestions for dealing with dealers and manufacturers; and details about how to sue in the courts.

The section that interests me most is titled "Last Resorts." It is useful because, as Nader and the other authors confess at the outset, the book is no panacea. "There are no easy ways to achieve" results, and quite often it is "last resorts" to which one is driven, after trying more conventional and polite tactics.

The best of the last resorts is picketing. If a car owner, after writing to the dealer, the manufacturer, a lawyer, public agencies, and Ralph Nader, is still stuck with a lemon and feels it is no fault of his own, he can put his complaint on a sign, attach the sign to the roof of his car, and park in front of the car dealer. As the authors put it, "This expresses your plight in a way that can't fail to bring a fast reaction. One owner reported receiving a full refund on his car as a result."

Sympathetic action by the car dealer is perhaps the simplest solution for all concerned. But the dealer may instead call the police, obtain a court order to stop the demonstration, or sue the picketer for damage to his business. In some states, including Texas and Oklahoma, courts have held in favor of picketers; in others, not. The right to picket in labor disputes and antiwar demonstrations has generally been recognized by the courts as a constitutional right, but consumer picketing is on shakier legal ground. In Massachusetts, Alabama, and New York, courts have told lemon owners to refrain from demonstrating.

In an Allegheny County, Pennsylvania, court, Book Chevrolet, Inc. brought a suit against a group called the Alliance for Consumer Protection and an individual purchaser who had picketed the dealer with the signs "Book Chevrolet Sells Rental Cars to Customers as Demonstrators" and "Book Chevrolet Uses Unethical Sales Practices." The individual defendant, Robert F. Fielding, and his wife had bought a 1970 Chevrolet station wagon, thinking it was a demonstrator. They later discovered that it had been a rental car. Fielding and ten or fifteen other persons staged a three-hour, peaceful demonstration in front of the dealership, neither obstructing traffic nor preventing anyone from entering the showroom. They justified their action as the expression of their constitutionally protected right of free speech. The court agreed that they were within their rights. The judge failed to rule on the merits of their complaint against the dealer or the dealer's assertion that their complaint was without foundation. But he ruled that there was no basis for enjoining them from protesting.

Nader, Dodge, and Hotchkiss recommend five guidelines for demonstrators, which will minimize one's chances of being sued:

1. Limit yourself to statements you can show are true.

2. Avoid statements that might be interpreted as attempting to coerce the dealer into a course of action or into paying you money.

3. Direct your disparagement at the vehicle, rather than at the dealer himself.

4. Do not interfere with the operation of the dealership's day-to-day activities (e.g. don't block his driveways).

5. Above all, don't interfere with the free flow of customers. Let them come to you or to your display.

What do you do when you've signed up for something you find you don't really want—for instance, a book a month by mail? The basic selling idea behind book clubs is that readers can save money by buying books purchased in volume by companies acting as middlemen. The clubs offer free books or bonus books as incentives for joining and continuing to buy. Everyone benefits. Publishers profit and are assured a minimum number of sales for selected titles. (Book-of-the-Month Club selections, it is said, are nearly always guaranteed best sellers.) The clubs take their own substantial cut of profits. And the reader gets books cut-rate, without ever leaving home or having to rummage for the ones he wants through the thousands of new volumes published each year. The rub comes when club members end up buying books they'd rather not have. Although they require subscribers to buy only an allotted number of books per year, most clubs send each monthly selection to each subscriber unless he mails in a refusal card.

Clubs are set up in a variety of ways to sell a number of products, including (in addition to books) records, flowers, plants, bulbs, meat, and miscellaneous gifts. Some require a minimum number of purchases; others do not. But intrinsic to most club schemes is the "negative option" sales concept. Only if the customer doesn't do anything does he receive merchandise. Negative option selling prospers because a substantial number of people, from 20 to 70 percent, regularly fail to reject items. Doing nothing is the easiest thing to do. Eventually one must pay the bill, but *that* comes later. Putting off payment results in a series of increasingly nasty letters demanding money.

Friends and enemies of negative option selling agree that if the practice were to end and club members were instead asked to exercise a "positive option" by sending in cards only for items specifically wanted sales would fall off precipitously. "The difference," an industry man says, "would be night and day."

Reputable book clubs—but not all book clubs—clearly and completely reveal the terms of membership; where negative option is used, the customer is told how it works. He is not, in other words, the victim of blatant deception. It is therefore not surprising, according to John Jay Daly, the vice-president of the Direct Mail Advertising Association, that of the millions of people currently enrolled in buying clubs, few complain.

The complaints Daly has seen more often relate to errors in computer billing or in mailing merchandise than they do to selling techniques. Besides, all book clubs will take a book back, he insists, if a member merely forgot to reject it in time. Daly claims further that people are often tickled pink to receive merchandise they thought they hadn't wanted, once they have it in hand. This is proved by a Michigan flower bulb company's survey, in which club members said they were delighted even with bulbs they had gotten by mistake.

Daly admits that a few companies may be a bit vague in their initial sales pitch. And his Association has tried to correct this by suggesting standard wording for advertising that would clarify the terms all clubs use in attracting members. The mailers' group began taking this new interest in reform just at the moment that the Federal Trade Commission began to poke into their affairs.

The FTC proposed that negative option selling be forbidden on the grounds that it plays on consumers' natural human tendency to forget things and to put them off. "Even explained clearly," said William Dixon, chief of the FTC division of trade regulation rules, "the method of selling is one necessarily designed to take advantage of these traits whether or not the consumer is that aware of it at the moment."

Any reforms proposed voluntarily by book and other clubs are a bit late, in view of the fact that Dixon says the Commission has been getting complaints since he came there in 1948. Letter writers are disturbed that they cannot extricate themselves from clubs once they've signed on. They charge that details of negative option plans were never disclosed or were too ambiguously stated to be understood. Members say they have received negative option cards just before the deadline for returning them—too late in effect to avoid receipt of unwanted merchandise; they say they have been billed for goods they have returned, or billed for goods they have already paid for, or billed for goods they never received. Some people complain that clubs haven't complied with the terms of bonus offers, that they have substituted books or other items for those advertised and ordered. People who aren't even club members write that they have received unordered merchandise. Dixon says that the interesting thing about most of the mistakes is that people end up getting something in the mail that they have to pay for. (Dixon himself belongs to both the Book-of-the-Month Club and the Literary Guild.)

Whatever becomes of the regulations, there are a couple of things consumers might mull over before joining clubs, particularly book and record clubs. The first is that if you live in an urban area and have available a discount book or record shop you can save about as much on your purchases as you can through a club, without any of the compulsions to buy, and you will have the satisfaction of doing your own selecting. The second is that no book club, as far as the FTC and the Direct Mailers know, has ever sued anyone for nonpayment of bills. The book clubs send out strong letters, but since the amounts of money involved are almost always small it is not feasible to go to court.

It is very unlikely that you would join any book or bulb or record club if your name were not on somebody's list. But it is, and you probably can't get it off. Not long ago, the FTC charged Metromedia, Inc., a communications conglomerate that sells mailing lists, with misleading 4 million persons who were sent out questionnaires promising an "opportunity to win fabulous gifts." They weren't told that the questionnaires were for the purpose of compiling mailing lists or that the assurances—"nothing to buy" and "no salesman will call on you"—weren't completely true.

The Supreme Court has upheld the Post Office's practice of allowing recipients of pornographic mail to have their names removed from offending mailing lists. Chief Justice Burger said in his opinion that a citizen's right not to receive mail he doesn't want takes precedence over a mailer's exercise of free speech in sending out unsolicited dirty mail. It's a tricky issue with a lot of implications for the junk mail business as a whole, not just pornographers.

The strength of the Post Office policy is that it allows individuals to decide for themselves what is offensive, which takes the Post Office out of the censorship business. If you are getting mail that you consider "erotically arousing or sexually provocative" and you don't want more of it, you may have it stopped. The Post Office will issue on request a Prohibitory Order requiring a mailer to purge you from his mailing list within thirty days or face legal action by the Justice Department.

The law is a powerful weapon against unwanted mail of all kinds. It takes initiative, but you *can* reject anything—magazine subscription letters, real estate opportunities, food ads—*anything* except perhaps a draft notice. (One young man tried to invoke the Pandering Act on his draft board, contending that he considered mail they were sending him the ultimate obscenity. The Post Office refused to issue an order.)

Previously, about the only thing one could do to get his name off mailing lists was to mark "Deceased" on the envelope and return it to the Post Office. To get temporary relief and at the same time sock the mailer with the return postage, he could "reject" a letter marking it "return to sender." If enough people did that, it would make direct mail advertising prohibitively expensive and might put a stop to it altogether.

There is some question about how unpopular junk mail really is. Many assume uncritically that everyone hates unsolicited mail from strangers selling merchandise, and that if people only knew how to do it they would stem the glut. Direct mail advertisers (which is what they prefer to call themselves) counter that theirs is one of the most effective advertising media. Using carefully selected mailing lists they are able to aim useful information about products and services to people most likely to be interested. Junk mail *sells,* and the mailers ask why, if people hate it so much, they read it and buy.

A lot of junk mail these days comes from real estate people selling vacation property beyond the city suburbs, where there are said to be fewer problems with pollution, crime, overcrowding, and race. All over the country, within weekend driving distance of big cities, there are cropping up country-club-lake-leisure communities, where small plots of undeveloped land are available next to new man-made lakes and eighteen-hole golf courses, approved by the Professional Golfers' Association. Here's your place for a second home, a weekend retreat, a vacation hideaway. Buying land gives a family country-club membership and country-club "status" for a few hundred dollars down and easy credit terms (at 10.2 percent simple interest). One company alone has more than fifty of these projects around the country in various stages of development.

Buying into the new carefree communities, however, may be just the beginning. Land is nearly always over-priced. In many cases the developers reserve the right to abandon the projects before the elaborate facilities they promise are completed. The land dealers who hint to white buyers that only token numbers of Negroes will be let in are having run-ins with the law. Percolation and other tests, required to establish that septic tanks can be put in and that water is there to be welled, are often fabricated by the promoters. In other words, the problems are never ending, and they begin with the first phone call or ad you get in the mail. The advertising schemes are often deceptive. They annoy the uninterested, and they add to the price paid by those who eventually buy.

One Washington, D.C., resident was contacted three times in a month by a Pennsylvania development. First he received a letter informing him that he had won a sweepstakes prize which he could pick up if he made a trip to the development. Once there, the letter said, he would get a check for five dollars (for his trouble) and a forty-five piece set of dinnerware. He would also get his sweepstakes prize and would be eligible for a discount of from fifty to five hundred dollars on the land, depending on his luck. The sweepstakes prize, he learned on visiting the project, was a free Florida vacation, which turned out not to include transportation or food—only a hotel room for two nights in another vacation development where another salesman would try to sell him land in Florida. The check for five dollars was good. The dishes were cheap plastic. And the hard sell was almost irresistible, with the five hundred dollar discount on the land that he "won."

He did resist, though, because he knew that the quarter acre he was offered for the low, low price of three thousand dollars had been bought from an orchard grower just months before for less than five hundred dollars. The purchase price, which had been outrageously blown up, included the cost of the expensive advertising and promotion. He also knew that the property report the project had filed with the United States Department of Housing and Urban Development contained the warning that the developer had posted no bonds and in no other way guaranteed that the improvements (a hotel, a lake, a new clubhouse) would ever be finished. And he learned that the developer, who said there was only one Negro family in the entire project, was being sued by the Justice Department for systematic discrimination under the Civil Rights Act of 1968.

The prospective buyer said "no thanks" and returned to Washington, grateful to be living in the city. But that wasn't the end of the tale. A week later a telephone solicitor, who obviously didn't know that he had already visited the place, called and offered to pick him up some Saturday in an airconditioned Cadillac limousine and drive him the seventy miles to Pennsylvania for a free lunch and a look at the same real estate. "No thanks," he said again. Still later, another salesman phoned to offer him a free dinner at a local restaurant and a slide show. This time, just to see what would happen, he told the caller that he was black and asked whether the company would sell to him. The salesman said there was no "policy" against it and promised to call back to confirm arrangements for the free dinner. He never did.

When the Justice Department brought suit against the company for racial discrimination, it went straight. Where once it advertised exclusively through the mails, using mailing lists carefully pruned of blacks and excluding black neighborhoods, the firm began advertising in Washington newspapers with a substantial black readership. It continued to use the mails too. The last offer I heard about was by far the most attractive. If you visit the project now with your letter in hand, you get a check for twenty-five dollars, no strings attached —except that those who end up buying land pay a heavy premium for the lavish and expensive advertising, the airconditioned Cadillacs, the plastic dishes, the free lunches, and the promises of clubhouses, airports, and lakes that may be mirages.

Ralph Gínzburg, the publisher, confided in me as he was preparing in 1970 to put out the first issue of a new consumer newsletter called *Moneysworth* that he recognized he would be using many of the same sorts of gimmicks to promote the sale of the newsletter that he would be disparaging *in* it. "I make no apologies for that because the marketplace is thoroughly corrupted," he said. "You've got to do certain things if you want to stay in business." (Ginzburg has since denied saying that, but he did say it.) It seemed to me particularly bold of him to put out a tip sheet for consumers, using devices he himself considered compatible with a corrupt marketplace. But at least he was being honest with himself. Ginzburg knows that merchandising is highly competitive and that to sell a product one must be able to establish to the satisfaction of the buyer that the product has desirable qualities, that there's a use for it, and that it is distinct from and preferable to other similar products sold by the competition. It should be established, furthermore, that the desirable, needed, quality product is either less expensive or a better value. You cannot live in a consumer culture and not know that such distinctions among products are often without meaning or truth. Salesmanship seems to require exaggeration. The man who makes the sale is usually the man with the best sales *pitch*. The actual properties of the product are another matter altogether, largely irrelevant to the selling. The growing consumer movement of the sixties and seventies aims to take the con out of consuming —to encourage accurate and fair claims for quality products and services, truth in lending, truth in advertising, and truth in packaging. An assumption of the consumer movement is that it should be possible to make a profit manufacturing and merchandising quality products that perform as advertised, that don't injure anybody when used properly, that contribute to rather than diminish the quality of life, and that don't harm the environment. But in our corrupted marketplace, it is a virtually untested assumption.

# index

17580

658.8
S

Sanford, David

Who put the con
in consumer?

| DATE | | | |
|---|---|---|---|
| Faculty | MAY 2 3 '74 | SEP 3 0 '76 | NOV 1 1 198 |
| DEC 4 '73 | SEP 2 3 74 | OCT 2 1 '76 | DEC 5 1980 |
| DEC 1 9 73 | JAN 2 4 '75 | NOV 2 4 76 | JAN 7 1981 |
| | | DEC 8 '76 | |
| JAN 5 | NOV 1 3 75 | JAN 3 '77 | JAN 2 1 1982 |
| JAN 2 8 '74 | DEC 9 '75 | JAN 2 0 '77 | FEB 0 8 1983 |
| APR 3 '74 | Jan DEC 5 '75 | MAY 2 0 '77 | |
| APR 2 4 '74 | JAN 2 0 '76 | NOV 2 '79 | |
| | | SEP 2 2 '80 | |
| MAY 1 0 '74 | MAY 7 '76 | OCT 2 8 1980 | |
| | | | |